GOD-SIZE YOUR CHURCH

GOD-SIZE YOUR CHURCH

*Beyond Growth
for Growth's Sake*

John Jackson

*Abingdon Press
Nashville*

GOD-SIZE YOUR CHURCH
BEYOND GROWTH FOR GROWTH'S SAKE

Library of Congress Cataloging-in-Publication Data

Jackson, John, 1961-
   God-size your church : beyond growth for growth's sake / John Jackson.
   p. cm.
   Includes bibliographical references.
   ISBN 978-0-687-64909-9 (binding: pbk., adhesive : alk. paper)
   1. Church growth. I. Title.

BV652.25.J315 2008
254'.5—dc22

2008040222

08 09 10 11 12 13 14 15 16 17—10 9 8 7 6 5 4 3 2 1

MANUFACTURED IN THE UNITED STATES OF AMERICA

Contents

Acknowledgments

I want to thank and recognize the many mentors who have shaped my life along the way. But, alas, it is impossible. Obviously, my parents and my family have continually sustained a huge impact on me. I was privileged to have many teachers, many examples, and many friends along the way. Pastors and writers mentored me without ever knowing it. Men like John Maxwell, Rick Warren, Bill Hybels, Jack Hayford, Andy Stanley, Ed Young Jr., Jimmy Evans, and a host of others have sown seeds into my life from up close and from afar. I once listed my favorite books and tried to stop at thirty but could not. Friends like Glenn, Ray, Scott, Tom, Dane, David, Tim, Andy, and others contribute to my life in a way that is hard to measure. My colleagues on staff and in leadership at Carson Valley Christian Center (www.cvcwired.com) have really written and shaped (and are shaping!) this story more than they will ever know. Paul Borden and the team at Growing Healthy Churches (www.growinghealthychurches.org) have helped us extend and "ripple" our story and my contribution to others. Ray Johnston and the leadership team at Bayside Church (www.baysideonline.org) have always fueled my passion for God-sized churches and belief in the miracle of "AND." The team at Abingdon Press has continued to be a rich source of encouragement and focus. So, anything good you see in here came from a stream of sources that can't be named. Any flaws you find in this book are mine alone.

As always, my wife, Pam, and my children Jennifer, Dena, Rachel, Joshua, and Harrison are at the center of my world next to Jesus. To them, I owe an amazing debt of gratitude for their love and care in my life. I want to acknowledge that Jesus Christ is the Lord of the church and of my life, and ultimately, anything of value here comes from His throne and His heart. My prayer is for you to God-size His role and impact in your life and the lives of those around you.

Foreword

I recently heard a pastor say, "We aren't trying to build a *mega*church. We want to build a *healthy* church." I thought to myself, "When did growth and health become mutually exclusive? Shouldn't the Christian church be both *growing* and *healthy*?"

The idea that there has to be a trade-off is business as usual in the church community—but *God-Size Your Church* makes clear that business as usual just isn't cutting it.

Need convincing? Just ask yourself a few simple questions:

- Why is the rate of population growth far outpacing the church's rate of growth?
- Why are 87 percent of Protestant churches stagnant or declining?
- Why did 50 percent of all churches in 2000 not add even one new member through conversion?
- Why are churches losing their teenagers?
- Why are so many Christians tippers instead of tithers?
- Why, if the doors were closed on many American churches, would the community never realize they were gone?
- Why are many pastors discouraged?

If you are asking questions like these—this book is for you. As I read *God-Size Your Church*, I thought, "It's about time!" A leader among leaders, John Jackson has delivered his most valuable book. He shows how it's possible to escape the tyranny of the "or" and pursue the boundless possibilities of the "and." A church can major in evangelism *and* discipleship. A church can develop devotion *and* help its community. A congregation can have both size *and* significance.

Years of coaching churches and church leaders make John uniquely equipped to offer both hope and strategic principles that will help churches of every size. This book is a must-read that will energize and equip leaders to build churches that are both growing and healthy!

Every church has scores of people needing a passionate leader to inspire them to God-first, God-honoring living. And every community has thousands of people disconnected from Christ, needing a high-octane church to demonstrate and deliver the good news. My prayer is that God will use this book to light some fires in you and your church that will never go out.

Ray Johnston
Pastor, Bayside Church
Granite Bay, California

1.

Why Not Order a Regular-Sized Church?

W ould you like fries with that? How about Supersizing your drink and fries for just forty cents more?" Supersizing a drink or fries seems reasonable to our fast food–addicted culture. But think about this: What if I asked you whether or not you wanted a regular or a Supersized church? How would you answer that question? What if I asked you about Supersizing your impact? Would you rather your church have a regular-sized or a God-sized impact in your community? Before you answer these questions, let me ask you one more. Do you think a bigger church always has a greater impact than a smaller one?

Church impact is often considered only from a numerical and program standpoint. A focus on numbers alone does not tell the whole story. There are many more dimensions than numbers to tell the story of what God is doing in your church and community. I believe that God-sizing your impact is all about the pursuit of a God-placed passion. I believe there is a God-sized impact for your church just waiting to break out in your heart, in the life of your church, and in your community. If you are passionate about fulfilling the Great Commission (and the fact that you are reading this book is a good indication that you are!), then you want to find the way to maximize the influence of your church and ministry in your community. God has given each of us an opportunity to lead and participate in a kingdom adventure. Our challenge is to fulfill the divine mandate He has given us. The Apostle Paul said it this way: "Do you not know that in a race all the runners run, but only one gets the prize? Run in such a way as to get the prize. Everyone who competes in the games goes into strict training. They do it to get a crown that will not last; but we do it to get a crown that will last forever" (1 Corinthians 9:24-25).

Not long ago, I was in Utah, finishing a day of teaching lay leaders from a denominational group about taking their churches to new levels of ministry. Then a unique question came to my mind. I'd already spent three hours with them and hoped I'd get a different answer, but the fact that I did not suggests how difficult the core issues really are. Here was my question—"If you were in the hospital today, how many of you would expect a visit from the senior pastor of your church?" That 80 percent of attendees immediately responded with that expectation is one reason that they are in churches with fewer than two hundred people in attendance each week. After some good clean joking about whether they really believed in the Protestant Reformation and the priesthood of all believers, we were able to discuss the difference between reaching more people for Christ and taking care of those already within the church family. (Full disclosure here: I am *totally* in favor of people being visited in the hospital; I just don't think it has to or should normally be the senior pastor of a larger church.)

Throughout this book, we will be on a journey of discovery. Many times we have come to believe that the community cannot be reached for Christ because of the hardness of people's hearts. Although that may be true in specific cases, another fundamental reality is often also at work. We reach our limit of being able to influence our town because we demand that our churches structure themselves a certain way, take care of each other a certain way, and conduct our ministry in ways that are most comfortable to us. Our journey of discovery here will force us to confront our core passions. Is it more important for us to have our churches meet our needs or have an effect on our community? *The choice of our strategic and ultimate values, rather than whether our churches are big or small, is the real issue behind God-sizing our churches.*

God-Size Your Church comes with a personal passion. I believe that God wants our churches to reach more people for Jesus Christ, to establish and secure them in their faith, and to equip them for kingdom work in the world. God longs for lost people to know Him and saved people to share Him with others: "So then, just as you received Christ Jesus as Lord, continue to live in him, rooted and built up in him, strengthened in the faith as you were taught, and overflowing with thankfulness" (Colossians 2:6-7).

This book not only comes with my personal passion for reaching lost people for Christ; it also comes out of my experience in starting a church in what I call a rurban community (rural on its way to urban). Carson Valley Christian Center (www.cvcwired.com) was started in 1998 after ten months were spent gathering a core. Now we are preparing to celebrate our tenth birthday. I fondly tell people that today we are living in and I am leading CVC 3.0. We have discovered a consistent need to develop and grow the ministry of the church as we move toward health. In fact, I'll take this opportunity to make a confession. For many years, I was so focused on reaching visible and numerical impact that I neglected some important but less visible aspects of health and lasting family and community impact (more on that later).

Today, I'm pleased to tell you that I see God at work in our church, making it a dynamic, growing, healthy, God-sized church in our community. I'm excited to share with you part of our story as we learn together how to lead and live in clusters of believers who are making a difference every day in their families, their work, and their neighborhoods.

Researcher Dave Olsen, in his book *The American Church in Crisis*, estimates that up to 94 percent of American churches are either at a plateau or declining in relation to population growth in their communities. If his research is true (and many other researchers agree with his numbers or suggest even higher levels of decline), then the American church is in trouble as it relates to how we reach our culture for Christ. But rather than giving in to despair, I think that God is even now beginning to show us what He has ahead for us. Several bright lights on the horizon will help us see God's plan for our ministries fulfilled in the coming years.

As you read this, God is right now beginning a movement of externally focused churches in smaller areas that are having a God-sized impact on their local communities. Pioneers in the megachurch movement like Willow Creek, Saddleback, Northpoint, and Fellowship Church paved the way. But today, many churches like Fellowship Bible Church in Little Rock, Mars Hill Church in Seattle, Mars Hill Bible Church in Grandville, Michigan, Perimeter Church in Atlanta, and a host of smaller churches like Hayward Wesleyan Church in Hayward, Wisconsin, Ripon Community Church in Ripon, Wisconsin, and the Rock Church in Sacramento are having God-sized impacts in their communities. My friend Mark O. Wilson has a blog (www.revitalizeyour church.blogspot.com/) devoted to encouraging pastors of small and rural churches, reminding them that small communities are no barrier to a God-sized influence. As he reminds his readers, "Your church can touch the world, regardless of your location. You can make a big difference right where you are!"

Many other churches are bringing us to a new horizon, a place where churches with a passion for impact believe God can bring more than just a regular-sized effect in their local communities. They believe He will create a God-sized church in their town. How about you?

2.

God-Size Your Church by Dreaming God-Sized Dreams

I first heard God speak the question, *Will you dare to dream big dreams for Me?* at a snow-covered church campground in March of 1996 at Greenlake, Wisconsin. My first response was no! I had been wrestling with God for quite some time about my future in ministry, but on that snowy day, I was reading the story of well-known church planter Rick Warren, in his book *The Purpose-Driven Church*, a story that I thought I was quite familiar with, given that we had lived in Southern California when Saddleback was first taking off. God seemed to be speaking into my heart as well. A dream of a local church that would reach unchurched people and change the world started to form. My initial icy response to God melted as the fire of passion began to burn in my heart.

Many of us are initially reluctant to dream big. Intuitively, we know that dreaming big most often leads to big change in our lives and ministries. And big change means risk, means stepping out of comfort zones, means climbing out of ruts. Yet I am convinced that God may be asking many of you the same question He asked me in 1996: *Will you dare to dream big dreams for Me?* I am praying that God will melt whatever icy responses may lurk in your heart and light His passionate dream for ministry instead.

Please do me two favors before you continue further into this chapter. First, dream a really big dream of what God could do if there were no obstacles in the way. Five years from now, if there were no limitations on finances, leadership, facilities, or programs, what could God do in you and through you to make an impact on the world through your local church? Can you see that picture clearly? What would worship look like? How would evangelism, discipleship, fellowship, and ministry take place? What life changes would people experience in the context of your dream? Make sure that you see every ministry dimension with some measure of clarity.

Now, take every dimension of your five-year dream and multiply it by a factor of ten. Let your spirit, heart, and mind soar as you consider what God could do that would be ten times your largest dream. If you are able to envision that, you just might be beginning to grasp what God is able to do when you raise your leadership lid and cooperate with Him in His agenda for your life. Take your vision and try to make it even larger. Will you dare to dream big dreams for God? If so, take another pass at your dream and God-size it!

Here's a well-known example of a God-sized dream that launched a God-sized church, Rick Warren's expression of "The Saddleback Vision" during his first sermon, March 30, 1980:

It is the dream of a place where the hurting, the depressed, the frustrated, and the confused can find love, acceptance, help, hope, forgiveness, guidance, and encouragement.

It is the dream of sharing the Good News of

Jesus Christ with the hundreds of thousands of residents in south Orange County.

It is the dream of welcoming 20,000 members into the fellowship of our church family—loving, learning, laughing, and living in harmony together.

It is the dream of developing people to spiritual maturity through Bible studies, small groups, seminars, retreats, and a Bible school for our members.

It is the dream of equipping every believer for a significant ministry by helping them discover the gifts and talents God gave them.

It is the dream of sending out hundreds of career missionaries and church workers all around the world, and empowering every member for a personal life mission in the world.

It is the dream of sending our members by the thousands on short-term mission projects to every continent.

It is the dream of starting at least one new daughter church every year.

It is the dream of at least fifty acres of land, on which will be built a regional church for south Orange County—with beautiful, yet simple, facilities including a worship center seating thousands, a counseling and prayer center, classrooms for Bible studies and training lay ministers, and a recreation area. All of this will be designed to minister to the total person—spiritually, emotionally, physically, and socially—and set in a peaceful, inspiring garden landscape.

I stand before you today and state in confident assurance that these dreams will become reality. Why? Because they are inspired by God![1]

Here is another story of a God-sized dream from Mike Holba, pastor of Ripon Community Church in Ripon, Wisconsin:

> The first time I experienced a God-sized dream coming to fruition, I was planting my first church in Ripon, Wisconsin. As we drove into the small town of Ripon, I never would have guessed that we were about to exchange our mini-van for a front row seat on a rollercoaster operated by God.
>
> When asked to describe our experiences planting a church here in Ripon, I often have said, "It's like having front row seats for a miracle." At least that's how I describe the good days. And on the other days, the ones when I am still trying to figure out what God is up to, I often have said, "It's like we are in the first seat of a rollercoaster car and God is operating the ride. Thrilling! Exhilarating! And yes, sometimes a little scary. But, because you have faith in the Operator, you know you will be safe."
>
> I would have never guessed as we drove into this 7,000 person town that we would have seen so many miracles, that so much would be possible. But God in His ultimate wisdom and holiness did. We began with no people, almost no money and very little experience. But we also had a simple desire to try to determine what God wanted and then do it.
>
> Genesis 6:22, *"So Noah did everything exactly as God commanded Him,"* became our special passage. I figured it worked out pretty well for Noah, so why not us?
>
> We began making plans and dreaming of what God might do. But I am slightly embarrassed to

admit that even though I am a dreamer and a goal setter, my dreams were way too "small town" for this tiny community. God's were huge!

With God at the controls, we simply targeted people who were turned off by church, but not by God and we went from 5 people (our family) to 100 in six months. Average attendance rose from 100 to 200 during the next six months and from 200 to 400 over the next few years.

At our first baptism service, we baptized 65 people in nearby Green Lake. The water was so cold that my surgically repaired knee was numb by the time I got out of the water. After 5 years, we have now baptized almost 3% of the city's entire population. Imagine the miracle of being involved in baptizing 3% of an entire community in just a few years!

Two hundred people participate in our small groups and we now provide food to nearly 400 people each month through our Thrift Store/Food Pantry ministry. We have also planted two daughter churches in other towns similar to our own.

The miracles that we have had a front row seat to witness are too numerous to list. Hundreds of people have now dedicated their lives to following Jesus. And the story of "Joann" is a testament to God's power in the life of anyone who is willing to open the door when Jesus knocks.

A few months before the church launched, "Joann" sent me an email saying:

"I am one of those people who is disenchanted with the church. I want to choose how much time I spend with church and do not want to be prodded into bible studies etc. I don't want people being judgmental and have not yet found a church that does not make judgments. I don't want a church to tell me how much money I should be giving. I don't want to feel like an outsider in a clique of Bible thumpers. I need a minister that I can feel comfortable bearing my soul to if need be. Do I sound hopeless—or like the average disenchanted church person? Please drop me an email. I will not be the least bit insulted if you tell me that I am climbing the wrong cross, and this church will not meet my expectations."

This might sound crazy, but I was so excited reading it! People like Joann are the reason we plant churches. She was exactly who I was looking for. Far from God at the moment, but full of potential. Joann has since given her life to Jesus, been baptized and has invited many, many people to attend. Her brother died recently and with my blessing, she conducted his memorial service herself.

After a very passionate message, she concluded her thoughts with the following statement:

"I don't know all of your beliefs. I know that everyone is in a different place and that's OK. Faith is a journey. Sometimes we stay on the road, sometimes there is a detour, and sometimes we're just lost. The important thing is that we eventually reach our destination. I believe that Jesus died for our sins. God's love for us is not earned, it is freely given."

Yes, considering her first email, I would call Joann's conversion a miracle. And despite my big dreams and plans, I never would have thought seeing so many of them in such a small town would be possible.

We have actually lived out Ephesians 3:20 over these last five years in tiny Ripon, Wisconsin of all places. And, there are now hundreds of people here that can quote that verse and say with belief, "To God be the glory" because of what He has done here.

The bottom line is, business as usual just won't cut it anymore. The church has been a bedrock foundation of Western society for hundreds of years, but today the church is standing on the edge of irrelevance. We need a fresh, bold, articulate vision for ministry that can be played out in local communities across the country. George Barna goes one step farther when he says, "Let's cut to the chase. After nearly two decades of studying Christian churches in America, I'm convinced that the typical church as we know it today has a rapidly expiring shelf life."[2]

Churches across America are grappling with barriers to their growth and questioning their viability in the future. Some researchers have suggested the U.S. alone experiences a net loss of 2,500 churches per year![3] During the past thirty years, American society has seen major social changes, one of which is the natural tendency toward large and small. The awkward middle-sized grocery store and church share similarities; they are too big to be small and too small to be big. These barriers are real, and they affect the ability of local churches to fulfill the Great Commission of Matthew 28:18-20 in their local communities. My passion in this book is to equip you to hear from God about your ministry and to go where He tells you to go. God-sizing is *not* about making your church a big church. It is about fulfilling the kingdom agenda of God in your community for His glory. God wants our churches to grow . . . to reach new people for Him and to influence our culture for Christ!

3.

Is God-Sizing a
Biblical Concept?

What if your church doubled in attendance in five years, baptisms increased by 400 percent in the same time period, annual income increased by the same percentage as did attendance, and you conducted and completed a building campaign, paying for the entire project with cash? You are a pastoral success, right? Your church is clearly a God-sized church, right? But what if during that same period your community did not change (divorce, suicide, and alcoholism rates stayed the same), total attendance in all churches of your community remained the same, and your people, when surveyed, did not have more of a biblical worldview or different moral behavior after being in your church two years than they did before being in your church? Now how do you feel about defining the success of your ministry?

Pastoral success is about rightly understanding, pursuing, and achieving what God's vision for your ministry is all about. God-sizing your church is all about hearing and pursuing that definition of pastoral success. For most of us, beginning to consider what God has for our ministries causes us to lean forward to the future and grasp what a church would look like that prevails against the forces of evil in our respective communities. Thinking about a local church that powerfully prevails against the presence of hell in its community is energizing. But most pastoral leaders have felt the opposite in our churches. We've watched, participated in, or led ailing churches that could use a strong dose of hope (or electric shock treatment!). Worse yet, we are clear that God is calling us to lead those same churches to health and vitality! Or perhaps, on the other side of the equation, you have observed a church that is big but seems hollow. You've wondered for years whether the church really was having the impact in the community that its attendance numbers seemed to indicate. Over time, you've pondered whether larger churches actually make a difference for Christ in their communities.

What if we could plant seed in such a way that the soil would bear thirty-, sixty-, or hundredfold returns? These are the dreams of church leaders who want to reach their community through God-sized *high-impact churches*. Let me elaborate with this definition that I developed years ago:

> High-impact churches break through spiritual, social, and leadership barriers to establish new churches and new ministries, and reach large numbers of new people for Christ. High-impact churches confront the law of inertia and the reality of human lethargy with a passionate, purposeful pursuit of God's plan for evangelism in their area.

Dreaming is fine, but reality must be faced. The truth is, according to the American Society for Church Growth (www.ascg.org), there is no county in America that has a higher percentage of churched persons today than a decade ago. (We believe CVC has now broken that statistic in our county, and we hear stories from other churches that are having a similar Supersize impact. Read our story in the next chapter.) I have personally heard C. Peter Wagner say it another way: "There are more churches on birth control than people!"[1]

So, why would anyone consider investing his or her life in the ministry of the local church? Only two phrases make the proposition worth considering: *Jesus Christ* and *Great Commission*. Jesus Christ, as our Lord and Savior, not only gave us the assignment of reaching and teaching people; He also gave us the vehicle with which to travel that road. In the local church one can know Christ, grow in Him, and experience all of God's family business. This book is all about helping your church have an impact for Christ in your world. I am passionate that we be clear about our calling to our particular "world" and that we make Jesus known in our area. Or as Perry Noble says, "We should make it hard to get to hell from our zip code!"[2]

Jesus said, "All authority in heaven and on earth has been given to me. Therefore go and make disciples of all nations, baptizing them in the name of the Father and of the Son and of the Holy Spirit, and teaching them to obey everything I have commanded you. And surely I am with you always, to the very end of the age" (Matthew 28:18-20). That imperative, known as the Great Commission, is the defining purpose of the church of Jesus Christ. Evangelism is the only thing that we are called to do here that we will not be able to do in eternity. For us to fulfill God's game plan for ministry, we simply have to make the Great Commission front and center of all we do. Churches with a God-sized vision for high-impact ministry in their community are fueled with passion for reaching people who are not in relationship with Jesus Christ.

Most of us would not argue with the notion that the Great Commission is at the center of the ministry of Jesus. It is true that we recognize the call for us, His followers, to follow that commission and reach people in order to make them His disciples. At the same time, we all know that there are so many competing activities and possible areas of focus for the local church that we often get off center from the Great Commission. If that commission is not at the center of the soul of the primary leader of the church, it will not be reflected in our DNA.

You cannot fake your vision "heartbeat." You can fake your sermon, you can fake that you care, but you cannot fake your vision. It has to be something that you, as key pastoral leader, breathe. If you can't breathe it and ooze it, don't do it! Once you are gripped by it, then "say it, spray it, wheel it and deal it until they feel it!"[3] The Great Commission has to flow from the heartbeat of the key leader and then ripple out in all that God has for us to do.

Until the key leaders of your ministry setting have made the soul-gripping decision to be an outreach-based church, the turmoil of tension between taking care of those already inside the family will constantly win over reaching those outside the faith. And that is a tragedy. One experienced pastor says it this way: "The church of our time and our place is largely inwardly focused. It has lost sight of the world outside its walls. Which is to say, the church has also lost sight of the God who works in and loves the world. And that is a genuine tragedy."[4]

So let's deal with the primary issue in God-sizing your church. Is bigger necessarily better? *No!* We want to move beyond mere numbers. A God-sized church is a place where people are being reached for Christ on the campus and in the community. Not only are people being reached; they are being transformed from living in darkness without Christ to living in the light of Christ. God-sized churches, regardless of the absolute number of the persons attending weekend services, are passionate to see lost people found, saved people growing, hurting people healed, and all people using their spiritual gifts for the glory of God. That is a God-sized church, and if it is not biblical, then we all are in trouble!

God-sized churches have a passion to see this biblical passage lived out in their midst:

> As for you, you were dead in your transgressions and sins, in which you used to live when you followed the ways of this world and of the ruler of the kingdom of the air, the spirit who is now at work in those who are disobedient. All of us also lived among them at one time, gratifying the cravings of our sinful nature and following its desires and thoughts. Like the rest, we were by nature objects of wrath. But because of his great love for us, God, who is rich in mercy, made us alive with Christ even when we were dead in transgressions—it is by grace you have been saved. And God raised us up with Christ and seated us with him in the heavenly realms in Christ Jesus, in order that in the coming ages he might show the incomparable riches of his grace, expressed in his kindness to us in Christ Jesus. For it is by grace you have been saved, through faith—and this not from yourselves, it is the gift of God—not by works, so that no one can boast. For we are God's workmanship, created in Christ Jesus to do good works, which God prepared in advance for us to do. (Ephesians 2:1-10)

As we see people transferred from the kingdom of darkness to the kingdom of light, the name of God will be lifted up in our communities, and we will see people drawn to Him through our churches, through our witness in the world, and through the power of changed lives. Now that is biblical!

God-Sizing Action Step:
Research Your Community

National statistics can be compelling; local statistics are more so. See how many of these questions you can answer for your particular community:

- What is the unchurched population in your community?
- By what percentage has the Protestant population in your community increased or decreased over the past ten years? How does that compare to the increase or decrease in the general population?
- What is the church-to-population ratio in your community? What was it in 1950?
- How many churches has your community gained in the last three years? How many churches has it lost?
- Read Matthew 28:18-20. If your church has a vision or purpose statement, how does it incorporate the ideas of the Great Commission? As you start a new church, how will you incorporate a Great Commission mind-set in those statements?

4.

The CVC Story:
Versions 1.0, 2.0, and 3.0

If you have a dream of your church becoming God-sized, it must be a dream that begins in the heart of God and catches fire in yours. I am praying and believing for you that you will have *His* vision for your ministry and your area. Whatever size church God is calling you to lead, it will come from His heartbeat and passion to see people connected to Him. Until you catch a God-sized dream and ride the wave of that vision, you'll not dare to dream for what He has in store for you.

During our first year at Carson Valley Christian Center, a man came up to me at one of our training events. He said, "I've listened to you, and I've watched what you're doing here. It doesn't look like you have a plan B if your strategy to reach the community fails." That man was a shrewd observer. I told him, "You're exactly right. We're completely committed to our vision, sink or swim." From the beginning, we determined to trust God for great things. We didn't *think* insignificantly, we didn't *believe* insignificantly, and we didn't *behave* insignificantly. I went to meetings of the Chamber of Commerce and told them our dream for our church to have a significant impact on the community. The risk was that I'd be laughed out of town after a couple of years if we didn't have that impact. This clear and singular vision for our church wasn't developed in a vacuum. God brought together a wonderful group of people who sacrificed time, money, and energy to invest their lives in reaching this area of Nevada for Christ. We all risked a lot. Now, after ten years of ministry here in northern Nevada, I believe we are seeing what God intended when He first birthed the vision in our hearts. Here is a little of our story:

I was born and raised in the home of an American Baptist pastor and his wife in Southern California during the 1960s and 1970s. Throughout my childhood, people patted me on the head and told me that surely "you're going to be a pastor just like your dad when you grow up." I'd grit my teeth and think, *Not if I can help it!* I wanted to be a professional baseball player, but at the age of fifteen I had a crisis when I realized that I wasn't good enough to play pro baseball.

The next six months were a searching time that culminated in a very clear call from God at age sixteen to pastoral ministry. I met the girl who was soon to be my wife, turned eighteen in July of 1979, married Pamela in August of that same year, and became a youth pastor at the First Baptist Church of Buena Park in September. I left Buena Park to become a youth pastor at Oxnard First Baptist Church (OFB) in January of 1981. This church was to become formative in my life, even though the experience was a roller-coaster ride! A master's degree from Fuller Seminary in June of 1983 was followed by a PhD in educational administration from the University of California in June of 1986. OFB went through a turbulent uproar the next year that, after a long and painful journey, resulted in my becoming the twenty-six-year-old acting senior pastor in late 1987 and then permanent senior pastor in mid-1988.

The years that I served at OFB are some of the sweetest and most painful of my nearly thirty years in ministry. Much growth happened, and yet there was lingering pain from the church difficulties of the earlier years. In October of 1992 I was chosen to be the executive minister of the American Baptist Churches of the Pacific Southwest (ABCPSW, now Transformation Ministries; see www.transmin.org); I was the youngest person in American Baptist history to hold that position. ABCPSW was the largest mission-giving region in the country but was in a terrible financial and confidence crisis. Baptisms had plummeted, and the churches were not confident about the future. God did a great work there over four and one-half years, and I thoroughly enjoyed working with the pastors and laypeople. I never did connect my heart with the national denominational bureaucracy, however, and kept feeling an itch to leave.

In March of 1996, God began to stir my heart toward church planting as we considered what it might be like to plant a church for people who believe the church is irrelevant to their lives but don't consider God to be irrelevant. On October 16, 1996, I resigned as the executive minister for the ABCPSW. Pam and I felt certain that God was calling us to plant a church in northern Nevada where only 5 percent of the population attended church in a given weekend. The call seemed certain, but the circumstances were odd. I had lived my entire life in suburban Southern California with millions of people. Northern Nevada—where we were heading—was what I call a rurban environment with only one hundred thousand people within thirty miles of our church plant.

I knew that God wanted us to develop what I later called a high-impact church that would quickly break through growth and community penetration barriers, but there were *no* Protestant churches with weekly attendance of more than three hundred people in our sphere of influence. We would need a team of committed people, lots of financial backing, and God's working in a powerful way, but we had no people, no money, and no clear indication of how God would do what we had come to believe He would do. I had experienced many churches imploding in their early lives because the leadership was insufficient for the ministry needs, and I prayed especially for a group of passionate leaders to emerge. God answered this prayer in a specific and tangible way.

My brother Gene and his wife, Barbara, committed early on to be part of the leadership team for the church plant. They had to move, leave a large church they loved (Eastside Christian Church in Fullerton), and sell Gene's business. Roy and Tracy Conover received our letter and told us they had been praying for a specific mission assignment. Both of them had participated in our youth ministry in Oxnard, had served in short-term mission trips, and had been part of a church plant (with some pain!) from Oxnard First Baptist. Not only were they called to join us and sell their home and quit their jobs, but it turned out they knew someone living in Carson Valley! Jacque and Cheri-Li Negrete joined us as soon as we moved here; they had actually participated in a church plant that we had done while I was the senior pastor of a previous church. The first leadership team of CVC was born: eight adults and twelve children made up the birthing coaches for the ministry.

Many stories of that early time revolve around the sacrifices of people from our Christmas card list (yes, we wrote the dreaded missionary letter, asking our friends and family for their support). Gordon and Freeda Manes (a couple in their nineties, living in Florida) stayed with our family when my siblings and I were young children. Although they had no children of their own, they stayed with us while our parents were on an extended trip. Gordon and Freeda live on fixed incomes, but they gave fifty dollars per month to a work they will never see to reach people they will never know on this side of heaven. Another young couple in their thirties, living in Spain with the Navy Seabees, gave twenty dollars per month after receiving our letter. More than fifty other people gave amounts ranging from ten to two hundred dollars each month. Every time a letter came in the mail it was a reminder of God's grace work in His people. It was also a sobering reminder of our accountability for God's work at Carson Valley Christian Center.

Shortly after arriving in Carson Valley in April of 1997, we began to plant the church. I think. Boy, was I confused. I left a busy office and a busy schedule to move to a new area with no relationships and no office. I remember sitting in the guest house on our property that was used as command central for the church. I had a game plan on paper. I had lots of dreams. But I had no people! How was a God-Sized church to be established with no people? One day I spent an hour with my neighbor (an unbeliever), just hanging out and talking. Then I left his home, saying, "I've got to get to work." God stopped me cold in my tracks. He said, *What do you think you have been doing?* Some church planter I was turning out to be.

After a month of getting settled, the three families who had moved to Carson Valley (the fourth family moved two months later) began meeting in a home group and developing relationships. Relationship building often meant going to the country store down the street (its former owners now attend our church), hanging around the post office or local McDonald's, and talking with repair people who would come to our house during the move-in process.

We spent lots of time in prayer and sharing those first few months before and after our move to the area. Faith Promise Partners living outside Carson Valley had committed more than two thousand hours of prayer per month; those in the core team also committed many hours of prayer within the early months of the church. Determined to hold a barbecue at our home in July of 1997, we invited every person we knew. That totaled about fifty people, including out-of-town relatives! A second barbecue a month later, at Gene and Barbara's home, drew eighty-five people. Each time we shared about the vision for a new church, we sensed that God was stirring up a number of hearts.

Other than Bible study, we committed to worship together at local churches. It had been my hope not to start a Sunday gathering until about three or four months before our February 1998 launch. As it turned out, most local churches in our area were uncomfortable with us attending, so on the last Sunday of July in 1997, we met at a Lazer Tag amusement facility with about twenty-five people. We started to meet each Sunday with one condition: *no non-Christians would be invited to these gatherings.* They were core-group meetings, not outreach events.

During this same time frame, God opened a miraculous door, and we were able to purchase thirty-nine acres of property in our target geographical area at a price well below the market price at that time.

Though we had about thirty-five people participating regularly by August, many of them had never been in a larger church, and I knew they really needed to see an example to grasp the concept. So, in September, we visited Bayside Church in Sacramento with twenty-three of our people. The senior pastor, Ray Johnston, gave us thirty valuable minutes in a local pizza parlor and answered questions. He gave us a high-impact takeaway idea: hold preview services to reach potential core group members, and do preevangelism in the community. In the two-hour ride back home, we decided that our first preview would be three weeks later.

Our first preview service, in September of 1997, started an awesome pattern. We had 145 people in attendance, and 12 of them prayed to receive Christ. Our first Discovery 101 class was held that day, with 47 attendees. For three weeks, we met in a casino/hotel in Minden and then moved to a Carson City casino, where we stayed four months. We had preview services in October (175 people) and November (202 people). Each time, more than 20 people joined what we called our launch team, and some people prayed to receive Christ. Discovery 101 classes were taught in the afternoon after each preview service, and we followed up with Discovery 201 and 301 classes. All services and classes were held in a section of the casino ballroom.

In the eight weeks prior to our launch, we really pushed our people and community toward the launch date of February 22, 1998. One hundred adults were on our team, and sixty-five of them had a specific service role in the life of the church. An enterprise can go public only once, so we went with all our hearts and souls. We used creative direct mail, newspaper inserts, posters, personal handout cards, and a variety of other outreach mechanisms to contact homes and businesses. We told all of our people that they were at a "terminal in Cape Canaveral": "We're launching a church instead of a rocket—and what you do in your role can make the difference in the entire project."

By January of 1998 we located a warehouse facility, and our local county affirmed our leasing of the facility on one condition: we had to secure a building permit at a cost of $100,000 and promise to complete our new facility on our land in twelve months. We pursued every alternative avenue, but it seemed clear that was to be our pathway (as an aside, I *do not* recommend building or buying anything in the first three to five years of a church start—it just happened to be God's provision and plan for CVC). In less than thirty days, we renovated 10,000 square feet of the empty 40,000-square-foot warehouse. One hundred adults and forty-five children assembled in the building one week before Launch Sunday.

On Launch Sunday, 424 people attended, and there were more than 20 decisions for Christ. We were ecstatic! The next eighteen months were a journey of God's continuous stretching of our faith and vision. At our first Easter service, 674 people attended, we added two services in June of 1998, and more than 1,300 people joined us for Easter services of 1999. We raised just over $300,000 toward the new building in 1998 and 1999, and we moved to our property in an 18,000-square-foot multipurpose building in October of 1999 because of pressure from our county to move out of our temporary buildings. We had a facility and land valued at $2.7 million upon move-in, and we owed $2.4 million. (Again, I do not recommend this!) We borrowed heavily from friends in ministry and were awed at how God kept meeting needs. Our key leaders sacrificed greatly to see these steps take place.

CVC was reaching 750 people in worship at the end of 1999, and by our second birthday in 2000, we were reaching 850 people each week. More than 2,450 people attended Easter 2000 services, and by May of 2000, CVC was averaging just under 1,000 people in attendance. Today, more than 1,800 people worship each weekend in a 650-seat auditorium on a 39-acre campus with 23,000 square feet under roof and more than 350 parking spaces in asphalt. In addition we have launched a second campus. We reach almost 2 percent of our surrounding population each weekend! Forty percent of the people who attend CVC each weekend were formerly unchurched. Many churches in our area have begun to grow as well. We feel that we've had a God-sized experience.

The Emergence of CVC 2.0

From that point on, things went well at CVC, at least on the surface. There were indications at the time that all was not well, but we had no idea what a deeper examination of our reality would reveal. In the summer of 2004, many staff members were tired and overwhelmed. I had a clear sense that many of them were almost paralyzed like deer in headlights. The idea of reaching more people just meant more work. Further, I was concerned that while our numbers were still strong, something was not right at the core. We continued to grow numerically until the spring of 2005, and then we hit what was to be our longest plateau and first decline up to that point. From the spring of 2005 until the fall of 2007, CVC actually reduced in size from its peak. Why did this happen, and could we have avoided it?

In hindsight, I think a variety of sociological factors were at work. In 2004 and early 2005 we were exceeding 80 percent capacity (what many experts consider the comfort level of most people in large-group settings) in both Sunday morning services, and though we still had room in our Saturday night services, people generally prefer to go at the "optimal inviting hour" on Sunday morning. Our key staff leaders were tired and frustrated by some of the more obvious barriers we were hitting. It took twenty minutes to clear out the parking lot between services (and we had only thirty minutes between services), and people were uncomfortably crowded in the hallways and children's classrooms. These were visible and frustrating barriers.

But several of us were convinced that other factors were at work. The more we evaluated our circumstances, the more we began to believe that we had inadvertently catered to and created a consumerist culture. People chose to participate in an ever-increasing amount of activity, but much of that activity did not directly contribute to spiritual growth. Further, the more we examined the six-year history of the church, the more we felt that we were not systemically creating disciples. Yes, there were real and glorious stories of life change. But from a systemic standpoint (see chapter 8 for additional details), we were failing to fulfill our mission of seeing unchurched people become disciples of Jesus Christ.

The Emergence of CVC 3.0

From 2004 to 2007, seven major staff people left. Six departures had to do with leadership, philosophy of ministry, or demographic issues in our area. The seventh staff member left because of a moral failure. Many among our church family, and particularly our staff and governing board, found this period very painful. For a great part of this time, I was reading John 15. There Jesus tells us that a branch that doesn't bear fruit will be cut off and a branch that does bear fruit will be pruned to bear more fruit. In John 15, Jesus tells His disciples that He has chosen them to bear fruit—fruit that remained. My clear sense was that we were not consistently bearing that kind of fruit in our first few years of ministry.

We are still grappling with the realities of what it means to be a God-sized ministry in our community. Developing disciples is a process, not a product, so we continue to ask God for wisdom and direction in our ministry. Part of my reason for sharing what is in this chapter is to reveal to you the source of my passion. My passion comes from my vision and from my pain. We have seen God at work among us in huge ways, and we have made some really bad mistakes. But each step of the way, we have sensed that God wanted a God-sized church in our community. The more I talk with people around the country, I know that He wants your church to move beyond numbers and to believe Him for life changes that bear fruit for His glory in the years to come. What motivates all of this? Here at CVC we have a fundamental commitment to the authority of God's word and the central priority of the Great Commission. We say that we're all about "friends helping friends follow Christ." That has become more than a slogan at CVC. We've tried to embed it into our DNA. The journey of these last ten years has been torturous in many respects. (More about that later!) However, we have been encouraged by hundreds of other churches and leaders who are watching God do His work in their lives and ministries. We are deeply passionate about helping churches and leaders experience the God-sizing of their churches!

5.

Four Ingredients to God-Sizing Your Church

Good managers organize for efficiency. Good leaders direct for effectiveness. Great leaders galvanize and mobilize for breakthrough. Great leaders take their teams to greater heights than previously thought possible. So, what does a great leader in a God-sized church do? I think great leaders have four jobs.

1. *Casting a vision.* Great leaders cast a vision of the future that is preferable to the present. Casting a vision is all about seeing the future with a God's-eye view and painting the picture in compelling ways that cause people to risk the security of today for the hope of tomorrow.

2. *Creating environments.* Great leaders establish a greenhouse for their teams where mission, vision, and values can flourish. Creating the right environment allows greatness to prosper; the wrong environment kills creativity and destroys dreams.

3. *Developing systems.* Great leaders don't just do pie-in-the-sky thinking. Great leaders deal with on-the-ground realities, and they create systems for relationships, process, and support mechanisms to further the life and vision of their organizations.

4. *Equipping other leaders.* Great leaders always multiply value in the lives of others by giving away leadership to others. Great leaders are not threatened by other leaders but instead are energized by them. Equipping others means the whole team grows toward the future.

The following chapters provide more details for each of the four roles as you endeavor to God-size your church while this chapter outlines each facet of effective leadership. You are in a position to influence change in your church. Your mastery of these four roles will equip you for effective ministry leadership.

First, leaders cast a vision. Casting a vision means that you are able to solidify the calling of God into accessible terms for your people. Part of what leaders do is to paint pictures, call forth emotion, and speak in sentences that sing rather than paragraphs that snore. I often find myself thinking that once I have shared a vision and put it into writing, people should just follow! Alas, it doesn't work that way. Having your heart captured by the heart of God and then translating that into terms that will connect your people with the known of today into the unknown of the future is a key task of the vision-casting leader. Further, you'll need to break through the cultural noise of your community so that people will be willing to sacrifice their time, comfort, and resources to be part of the vision.

Second, leaders create environments. Creating environments is about recognizing the significance of venues and spaces where people can connect. People long to belong. Church leaders who recognize the importance of environment will create a spectrum of opportunities. When I teach on these principles, I often use a continuum that ranges from anonymity to accountability.

People want some environments where they can maintain *anonymity*. They ask, "Will my needs be met here?" or more precisely, "What's in it for me?" After people experience an environment where they can feel safe, they then ask the second question: "Is there anyone here like me?" That is the question of *affinity*. Do you have environments where people can discover their affinity with others? Even if I discover that we have affinity, I still have another question, "Are you who you seem to be?" That is the question of *authenticity*. I want to know that you can be trusted and that you are who you say you are. Do you have environments where people can experience authenticity? Finally, I decide whether I am willing to trust you. *Accountability*—living as a true brother or sister in Christ and participating in the ministries of the church—almost always flows from environments that have made it possible for people to flow from a state of anonymity to affinity to authenticity. I will trust you if I believe in you. Do you have environments where trust and accountability are encouraged?

Third, leaders develop systems. The human body is a glorious example of simplicity and complexity. God has designed the physiological structure of our humanity to be an interwoven set of complementary systems. Ephesians 4 is clear that His divine design is for each individual part to work properly with the others. Your church should have systems to attract and reach out to people, connect them to God and one another, and help them grow to spiritual maturity through discipleship, serving in ministry by using their spiritual gifts, and reproducing themselves by reaching out to others. Does your church have the proper systems to fulfill the vision for God-sizing your church?

Fourth, leaders equip other leaders. God-sizing your church will always require more and better leaders than if you simply "do laps" and continue everything the way you have always done it. I heard Wayne Cordeiro of New Hope Christian Fellowship in Hawaii say, "Everyone is a ten somewhere" within the body of Christ.[1] Developing your team means that you will learn to *release* others for ministry roles for which they have been gifted, *resource* them for the tasks that they will need to accomplish, and *rejoice* in their success in ministry. Yes, doing all of this requires personal security on the part of the senior leaders, but I think it is thoroughly biblical! Some churches depend on the pastor to be the source of every vision, every activity, and every decision. That's not the way churches that want to be God-sized work, and it's not the model I see in the New Testament. I believe that the role of the senior pastor is to hear from God and provide overall direction and vision to the church family. In addition, leaders desire to build a culture where persons want to pursue God with all their hearts, souls, minds, and strength so each one fulfills his or her God-given assignment within God's kingdom. "Everyone is a ten" is a full-employment policy in the kingdom of God, and it is essential for God-sizing your church.

God-sizing your church begins in the heart of the senior leader, but it quickly spreads throughout the church leadership. It is my prayer that God will begin to stir in your heart an understanding and a passion for what it could look like for your church family to influence your community for the glory of God. What would it look like if you had clarity about His vision for the ministry? What if you had confidence in the environments that help people move from anonymity to accountability? What if the systems of your church were healthy and helped ensure that you knew how to monitor health within the church? What would happen if leaders were raised up, resourced, released, and rejoiced over as they experienced the hand of God upon them in their newfound passion for serving Him? Let's take the journey together in these next few chapters and move from imagination to application.

6.

God-Size Your Vision

How, exactly, does God-sizing your vision work in a local church? Several years ago, I developed a graphic that I have since used to teach this process all over the United States and in Kenya, where I have been privileged to do leadership teaching. Essentially, the process involves three steps: we are gripped by God's call, we grasp the needs of our community, and we recognize the gifts within our church family. This cycle begins when we are first gripped by the vision, but it is often repeated over time in the development of the ministry.

God's vision for your ministry must grip your soul before it can grab the heart of anyone else. Vision casting must begin in the heart of God. Only as you grapple with what He wants in your life will you be able to move into the new and challenging dimensions of ministry that He has for you. A church's vision must be clear if the church desires to be a vital place taking new ground in the battle for people in your community. If the vision is not spelled out and outreach oriented, your church will face a growth barrier of significant size.

Once you have been *gripped* by God's vision for you and for your ministry, you can start to see the needs of the community and *grasp* those needs with new God-sized eyes. *God-sized churches have a heart for reaching*

Figure 1
The Vision Cycle

Gripped
by God's Calling

**VISION
CYCLE**

Recognize
Gifts

Grasp
Community
Needs

people for Jesus Christ. If your vision is to care for the contented, then you will not produce passion in your people to reach those outside the boundaries of the church family. Walt Kallestad's book *Turn Your Church Inside Out* is an easy read and a compelling reference for helping you and your church make clear its vision to reach unchurched people. All churches recognize that everyone needs to come to relationship with Jesus Christ. At the same time, each church that wants to be God-sized will look for tangible ways to be Jesus with skin on in its local community in order to reach people and bring them to Christ. For example, one exciting dynamic of having a clear outreach-oriented vision is recognizing the need to be present in the community. Rather than wait for the community to show up on the church's doorstep, God-sized churches are both attractional and missional (they attract people to them, and they go to where the people are to reach them). Sometimes in the current church leadership conversation it seems as though we have forgotten about the miracle of *and*. Your church can and should be attractional *and* missional. It should reach lost people for Christ on your campus and in your community. Your God-sized vision will lead your church to draw the community to you and to take the good news of Jesus Christ to them as well.

God is calling your church to attract unchurched people in your community and to reach out in ministry to your community. Some call this presence evangelism, being present in the network of society, being present in the ministry to physical needs of people, and being present in the spiritual battle for people's souls. Gary McIntosh and Glen Martin did an excellent job of observing this when they wrote, "Churches that are effective reaching people for Christ see the needs of the unchurched, establish ministries that allow the church to be present in the community, and have a process by which they are able to draw these unchurched people into the safety of Christ and a local church."[1]

If you have been *gripped* by God's vision for you and your church, if you have then *grasped* the specific needs of your community through which you can reach people in the name of Christ, then you will have to understand the *gifts* that God has entrusted to you and to your leadership core. Developing a group of committed core people who share your heartbeat for the vision, who have passion for the community, and who recognize the gifts that God has entrusted to the church family is key to the health of a God-sized church. In fact, a healthy church must have its core leadership in unity over the vision, in harmony with one another, and in commitment to the focus on ministry to the community. Larry Osborne's book *The Unity Factor* makes the point that churches that push forward with programs, activities, and structure without unity do so at their peril. Countless stories of church division and difficulty can be told about churches that never arrived at unity of purpose and vision. A growing church will be led by a leader who understands the imperative of developing unity and cohesiveness among the key leaders.

Recognizing the gifts that God has entrusted to your team will then equip your leadership team to develop your specific plans for ministry. In almost all circumstances, you will need to focus on basic core ministries (worship services, small groups, children's and youth ministries) as foundational. As you trust Him, He will show you the key leadership people for these core ministry roles. In addition, however, God will link your vision and passion for ministry, and your understanding of the key needs in your community, to give your ministry a distinctive approach in your community. For instance, CVC has long recognized the importance of the performing arts in our local community. We have regularly prayed and tried to make space for artists and the performing arts to grow in our church. As I write this, we are preparing a glorious offering of the arts to our community that we believe will reach many for Christ. That would not happen if we had not recognized and made space for the gifts that we believe God wanted to lift up among us.

Casting a vision is critical to God-sizing your church. It is not about being large. It is about being full of passion. If you are passionate about God's call and are gripped by it, if you are sensitive to and grasp the needs of your community, if you are prayed up, and if you recognize and call forth the gifts of your leadership team, God will grow your church. God will allow your leadership to influence your community in a way in which He receives honor. I believe in what God longs to do in and through you, and it all begins in the heart of God for you and for your ministry. Go hear from Him and then lead your people into the center of His heartbeat for your church and community!

7.

God-Size Your Environments

An effective leader understands the importance of creating God-sized environments. In my experience, four key factors in creating God-sized environments affect our ability to reach our communities: (1) understanding the community you seek to reach; (2) creating weekend worship environments that connect with the community; (3) developing special events that appeal to the community and provide special invite-and-serve opportunities for your people; and (4) designing spaces where people can connect in relationships to one another and encourage spiritual growth. Each of these four environmental factors is essential to building a healthy church family.

(1) *Understanding the community you seek to reach.* God-sizing church leaders are effective students of the culture of their community. Sometimes it is helpful to review basic information (for instance, visit www.zipskinny.com for your zip code to compare a variety of factors in your local area), and it is always imperative to pray that God will give you spiritually discerning eyes to understand the reality of your area. When you are God-sizing your church, look at several aspects relating to the context and conduct of your ministry. Of greatest importance is understanding the living, breathing texture of the fabric of your community.

You must learn to exegete your culture as you do the Scriptures, since you are engaged in a missionary task as a leader of a God-sized church. What are the factors that influence the people who live in your area? What are the everyday personal, family, economic, social, and spiritual pressures of people in your community? God-sized ministry always finds a way to connect with the community and meets needs in the name of Jesus. Are you a student of the community where God has called you, and do you know how God has specifically called you to create environments to meet those needs?

(2) *Creating weekend worship environments that connect with the community.* Ed Young of Fellowship Church in Dallas (www.fellowshipchurch.com), in his monthly leadership CD series titled *Leadership Uncensored,* says, "It is all about the weekend, stupid." At our church in northern Nevada, we modified Ed's saying a little: "It all starts with the weekend." Churches that God-size their ministries will be acutely aware of how their weekend services connect with people and help them move toward life in Christ and spiritual health. Understanding the community and ensuring that the weekend services help people connect the timeless and eternal truths of God's word to the daily reality of their lives are important parts of God-sizing ministry. Further, being able to help people experience and encounter God in an environment of worship and biblical community is central to a vibrant church life. We took some principles of *The Purpose-Driven Church* by Rick Warren and ultimately developed our model to visualize what it looks like to move people through a variety of environments toward spiritual health and maturity. Here is our diagram as it now exists:

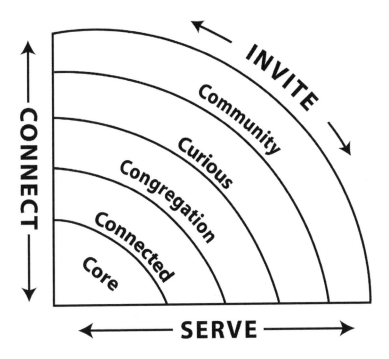

Figure 2
**Moving people through a variety of environments
toward spiritual health and maturity**

Each of our designations in the diagram (Community, Curious, Congregation, Connected, Core) relates to environments we have designed to help people move from the weekend services into deeper relationships and the fulfillment of God's plan for their lives. Have you designed your weekend worship services in such a way that you are helping people connect to God, His word, and His plan for their lives?

(3) *Developing special events that appeal to the community and provide special invite-and-serve opportunities for your people.* Big events provide a tool for reaching a broad

spectrum of your local community. In each community, there is a natural rhythm to the year, and most likely, there are natural events that your church can connect with or partner with in order to reach the most people for Christ. Our local community plans numerous events around the Fourth of July, but everything is quite costly. To have the broadest outreach potential and make a positive touch in our community, we determined to schedule a Fourth of July event earlier in the day and to make the event completely free. We focused the event on young families without competing with the other events in the community. Over time I have become convinced that this event has provided a special link for our people to invite (and inviting someone to a special event rather than a weekend worship service is often an easier first step) and to serve the community. Do you have any specially designed outreach events that help your people reach, invite, and serve your community?

(4) *Designing spaces where people can connect in relationships to one another and encourage spiritual growth.* God-sized churches provide environments where people can know one another, challenge one another to grow, and encourage healthy spiritual habits. When a ministry begins to influence the culture, the community, and the crowd at the weekend services, God-sizing leaders develop environments where people can be in biblical community with one another. One study of effective churches concluded, "Effective churches have specific ministries designed to help people break down the walls of confrontation, isolation, stagnation, and fragmentation. These ministries make the people accountable to one another and urge the people to continue to move forward in their growth."[1] Are there groups, classes, teams, and contexts where people can grow in their relationships with God and with one another as a fundamental part of their spiritual journey?

God-sizing churches have become creative design centers. Yes, they call the people to worship, to repentance, to discipleship, to ministry, and to holiness. All these happen in healthy God-sized churches. God-sized churches have determined that they will constantly move toward life and health through creating environments where vitality and growth can occur. Leaders of God-sized churches are equally passionate for evangelism and discipleship, and they recognize the imperative of creating environments that accomplish these purposes.

8.

God-Size Your Systems

The third task of an effective God-sizing leader is the development of systems that support the mission, vision, and values of the organization you are leading. Alvin Toffler, the author of *Future Shock*, said, "You've got to think about big things while you're doing small things, so that all the small things go in the right direction." To facilitate the God-sizing of your church, it is imperative that you think about the systems of your church family *now*, while it is small, in order for things to go well when it grows bigger. A. A. Milne, creator of Christopher Robin and Winnie-the-Pooh, provides my favorite definition of *organization*: "Organizing is what you do before you do something, so that when you do it, it's not all mixed up."

In our context, we at CVC have a vision for spiritual transformation. Our slogan is "Friends helping friends follow Christ." We have created three primary systems to support that vision: inviting systems, which provide an opportunity to reach people for Christ; connecting systems, which engage people in authentic relationships for spiritual health; and serving systems, in which people discover their spiritual gifts and develop their leadership skills.

In *The Very Large Church*, Lyle Schaller explains that social environments have become much more complex, anonymous, and hostile. Larger institutions are in the fabric of our society; therefore, larger churches are an increasing presence in our world. Since "large" is such a part of the social landscape, Schaller suggests that we need large churches to significantly connect with those born after 1965. One of the realities of larger organizations is that they are complex; similar to the human body, they are a set of interrelated systems. God-sizing leaders will lead their churches or ministries to develop systems to accomplish the vision that God has given them for their organizations.

When thinking about the systems of a church family, it has always seemed to me that we should think of the human body, since God designed it with several major systems, such as the circulatory, digestive, and immune systems, to work together. God is the master system designer, whether in the human body or in the church, the body of Christ. Each body system serves a necessary and specific purpose, is interrelated with the other systems, and is essential for health. I believe the church also has a number of specific ministry systems, essential for a church to become a fully functional biblical community of faith. Based on my almost thirty years of pastoral, denominational, and leadership experience, I believe the necessary systems in a church include the following:

- an *evangelistic* system to help your people reach other people for Christ
- an *assimilation* system to help connect new people to the life of the church family
- a *discipleship* system to help grow people from spiritual infancy to spiritual maturity
- a *healing* system to help people become free from the bondage of the pain in their lives
- a *ministry* system to help people discover and use their gifts to serve others for the glory of God

- a *mission* system to help mobilize Christ followers to serve their communities and the world as Jesus with skin on

It is beyond the scope of this book to fully detail each system, but I will explain a bit about how each of them functions in a God-sized church. In addition, I want to be clear that while I have not detailed a system for the people of God gathering together corporately for worship, I am deeply committed to the essential nature of the gathering of the local church assembly for worship to connect our hearts to God, for teaching to connect our minds to God, and for ministry to equip us for living out our faith in everyday life. A church that is faithful in worship and gathering together establishes the foundation for God-sizing the ministry through the various systems of a healthy church family.

Evangelistic System

A church with a healthy evangelistic system will consistently lift up the heart of God to reach people who do not know Christ. There are any number of ways for a church to cultivate an evangelistic heart, but most effective systems about evangelism are built on the pillars of relational evangelism, invitational evangelism, and missional outreach. In relational evangelism, church leaders equip people to naturally and comfortably share their faith with persons they know who have not been introduced to Christ. Invitational evangelism creates the system where people are equipped to invite their friends and circle of influence to services, activities, and events at the church so that they can then come to know Christ. Missional outreach is about being Jesus with skin on in the local community by responding with acts of compassion, justice, mercy, and kindness to the direct needs of people as a way to demonstrate the love of God. A God-sized church will consistently address the evangelistic temperature of the church culture to have it burn hot like the heart of God.

Assimilation System

God-sized churches have a passion for connecting disconnected people. Community Christian Church (www.communitychristian.org) in Naperville, Illinois, has as its mission statement, "Helping people find their way back to God." Part of living out that vision is helping people connect with the faith community through small groups. A fully functioning assimilation system helps connect people to God and the community of faith, typically through offering an introductory class, providing follow-up mechanisms, and integrating people into small groups or classes at the earliest possible time. For many people, the easiest door out of the church is a huge back door because they have never been properly connected. God-sizing leaders looking for the best reference work on assimilation should check out *Fusion: Integrating Newcomers into the Life of Your Church* by Nelson Searcy and Jennifer Henson. Leading a God-sized church means developing a proper assimilation system to ensure that people are connected.

Discipleship System

Attracting people to the community of faith is not the primary aim of any God-sizing church. The primary focus of every biblical church is to see the fulfillment of the Great Commission in Matthew 28:19-20, where we are commanded to "make disciples." Willow Creek Community Church in Chicago (www.willowcreek.org) has for years held up the mission statement "to turn irreligious people into fully devoted followers of Christ." The mission statement of my church is to see "unchurched people become disciples of Jesus Christ," and our vision statement is all about the "spiritual transformation of Northern Nevada and the Mountain West." A discipleship system that is working well is able to bring someone from spiritual infancy to spiritual maturity through a process of study, relationships, mentoring, and mastery of truths and practices central to the faith. A recent study, REVEAL (www.revealnow.com), unveils several of the most effective discipleship steps that churches are using today.

Healing System

People are messy. We are broken at the core and in need of a Savior and a Healer. Jesus Christ longs for us to be free from the pain of our past and the imperfect reality of our present, and to give us hope for the future (Jeremiah 29:11). A God-sized church provides a variety of care systems to ensure that people can be loved, encouraged, and challenged, and receive healing from the hand of God. Most of these healing systems are within the connecting environments of the church where specific ministry can happen within small groups or very personalized settings.

Ministry System

The Bible teaches very clearly that every Christian has at least one spiritual gift (1 Corinthians 12:4-11) and that God has placed us strategically within His family so that we can contribute to the proper working of the whole by doing our individual part (Ephesians 4:1-16). Discovering our spiritual gifts in order to find what God wants us to do and where God wants us to serve is important in an effective God-sized church. Making sure that people know and understand their gifts and that they are on the field instead of on the sidelines is part of the core message of two excellent resources: *The Purpose-Driven Church* by Rick Warren and *Doing Church as a Team* by Wayne Cordeiro.

Mission System

For far too long, churches have often invited people to "come and see us." Today, many God-sized churches recognize the need to be Jesus with skin on in their local communities and around the world. Matthew 5:13-16 exhorts us to be salt and light and live our lives in such a way that people see our good works and glorify our Father in heaven. Ephesians 2:10 tells us that God actually prepared good works for us before the foundation of the world. A God-sized church views the needs in the community as opportunities to touch hurting and wounded people with the love and kindness of Jesus. When the life of Jesus gets lived out locally and globally, the church will become more like Christ, and the communities will be drawn to Him.

Each system referenced above is a key piece of an integrated whole. Remove one of the systems, and the church family will not grow in a healthy and God-honoring way. In my experiences, when churches I led did not properly conceive or execute one of the essential church systems, the results were always demonstrated by our ministry missing the mark in tangible ways. Our ministry did not produce healthy people, and it was clear that our church would never produce the kinds of leaders we needed to take us to the next levels of ministry. The next chapter will help us God-size our leadership-equipping systems to develop healthy disciples of Jesus Christ.

9.

God-Size Your Leaders

Athletes and entertainers structure their lives for peak performance, but the body of Christ often functions in a very different way. Athletes eat right, exercise religiously, and tone their bodies so they are at their optimum efficiency on the day of the event. In the same way, entertainers practice for hours and prepare with others in the band, symphony, or group so they are at their best when the lights come on and the crowd cheers. Whether the rewards are tangible (financial or public acclaim) or intangible (pride of accomplishment), peak performers aim for success and structure their lives and efforts to achieve optimal output.

In the church, however, instead of preparing people for peak performance, we often use people to fill positions in an organizational chart we have developed. When we need a second grade teacher for Sunday school, we find somebody—anybody!—who will say yes. We need a different value system. We need to help people find the place where they can fulfill their calling, serve in their area of giftedness, and see God use them in their sweet spot. We need to inspire people to excellence instead of using them to fill empty slots.

God-sizing leaders cast visions, create environments, develop systems, and equip leaders. Most church leaders recognize the importance of equipping leaders, but are vexed by the actual experience of doing it. In this chapter, I want to explore four specific practices that will help you equip leaders on the way to God-sizing your church: life on life, skill training, benchmarking, and leadership development.

Life on Life

Equipping, at its core, is about relationships. It takes time to shape and speak into the lives of others while they are being grown and developed as leaders. The only way that I know to sow hope and truth into a life is to do life together. Relational shaping involves formal and informal times together, much like the development of a healthy relationship. In some ways, the equipping journey is a combination of parenting, dating, marriage, and team sports! By the way, *every* time I've had a leadership failure on my teams, it has been due (at least in part) to the fact that we didn't stay connected life on life. This, of course, raises the issue of how many people you can equip at one time. The answer varies, but if you are talking about intensive equipping, the number is fewer than you think (especially if you are a Commander-style leader; see my book *Leveraging Your Leadership Style* to explore that subject).

To facilitate life-on-life equipping, various teams in our church do the following, among other things:

- We go out for coffee or juice with no formal agenda.
- We spend time in each other's homes.
- We have recreational fun together.

Invest time in your team members by doing life together with intentionality, and you will become a better leadership equipper.

Skill Training

One meaning of the Hebrew word for training is "to make narrow." Skill training helps provide skills and strategic understandings for application in specific contexts. Since vision is always more caught than taught, the process of training often provides great vision-refining moments. Given the abundance of training opportunities available to us in our modern American society, I think there really is no excuse for not sharpening the specific required skills for your team. A benefit of training together is that we learn better when we can recognize the differences in our various learning styles and appropriate what comes naturally to others. Effective training takes place when teams sharpen the skill sets of team members and increase both productivity and synergy by most effectively using the resources and talents of team members.

Benchmarking

At its worst, benchmarking is simply "monkey see, monkey do." If I see something good in another church, then I can ape it in my church. That is a terrible approach to equipping leaders. At its best, however, benchmarking is valuable because it exposes your leadership team to greatness and sparks discussions about how your church might carry out ministry more effectively. Visiting other churches that are doing a noteworthy job in ministry can elevate the thinking of everyone involved. Whenever I have the privilege of speaking to other teams, I strongly encourage them to develop the habit of visiting other God-sized churches in order to learn and be challenged by them. At one point in the life of my organization, we provided funds so that in addition to our regular conference events, each member of our pastoral team could visit at least two other churches annually to learn their stories and benchmark their ministry practices. Another way to benchmark at a distance is to identify fifteen to twenty key church websites and visit them on a regular basis to see what is new and exciting. I encourage the leaders with whom I work to keep churches that are at least double their size on their radar screens in order to learn from those who have had to scale their systems to serve larger groups of people. We are always trying to equip our leaders to be lifelong learners. Leaders who are not learners are not leaders for long!

Leadership Development

It has been my privilege to teach leadership here in the United States, as well as in Mexico, Spain, and Kenya. Many of us want to believe that leadership is about position and performance in a specific context. But both Jim Collins and John Maxwell talk about levels of leadership. We must teach people that leadership is a process, *not* an event. Equipping leaders to understand and experience the full measure of their leadership potential over time is an essential part of the leadership development process. The contrast between leaders who understand their responsibilities (tasks, process, organizational duties) and those who understand the importance of developing themselves, their people, and their shared vision is huge. Leadership development results in long-term multiplication of leaders rather than a static state of leadership supply. To develop leaders effectively, we must commit to leadership as a process and help people become lifelong learners.

God-sized churches see to it that people have shared experiences of working together, facing challenges, cultivating vision, and deepening their relationships with Christ and one another. Leadership equipping is not a solo sport! Effective leaders equip other leaders. That equipping ministry produces a ripple effect that reaches the shores of heaven. The Apostle Paul was clear about that in 1 Thessalonians 2:19-20 when he wrote, "What is our hope, our joy, or the crown in which we will glory in the presence of our Lord Jesus when he comes? Is it not you? Indeed, you are our glory and joy." At our church, we say, "Changed lives are our business." We've learned over time that equipping leaders is a core technology at the heart of our business!

Noel Tichy of Harvard has written in *The Leadership Engine* that GE's leadership-equipping process was a major force in its long-term consistent record of growth under Jack Welch (and now Jeffrey Immelt). Creating a steady stream of emerging leaders is a must for a God-sized church. Since all business is ultimately about people, we need to be willing to develop, care for, and cheer on the success of those who work with us, for us, and around us. Andrew Carnegie said his desired epitaph was, "Here lies a man who attracted better people into his service than he was himself."[1] Cultivating a life and a ministry that are inherently relational will improve your emotional health and will enhance the fruit of your labor as you lead your church to becoming a God-sized church.

10.

Barriers to God-Sizing: Your Frying Pan Is Too Small!

One day, Frank went out fishing. He established himself on one side of the lake as he noticed another man fishing on the other side. For the next three hours Frank had zero luck (he was getting skunked, as they say in fishing lingo). What was more frustrating was that he saw the guy on the other side of the lake pulling in fish on a regular basis. Even worse, the guy was throwing back the *big* fish he caught. Frank finally had enough! He marched over to the other side of the lake to ask the guy what bait he was using. The stranger told Frank that he was using worms grown naturally on his farm with a special mixture of soil and food. Then Frank asked him his real question, "I've been watching you for three hours. Why in the world are you throwing back the largest fish you catch? That is so frustrating for me to watch!"

"That's easy," the stranger replied. Pulling a small frying pan out of his backpack, he said, "My frying pan is only this big."

Many of us have stopped fishing for bigger fish because our frying pans are too small. We limit ourselves to our current reality and shape our ministries around that, rather than freeing ourselves to dream God-sized dreams. Fishermen with a frying pan problem are not the only ones with limits on their ability to reach new heights for God, however. Consider Stewart.

Stewart is a runner. Actually, he is a jogger, but he says he is a runner because it makes him feel better about himself. One spring, after a harsh winter when he celebrated the holidays a bit too heartily and almost ate himself into oblivion, he took up running to burn off the hibernation insulation around his waist. *This year is going to be different,* he thought. *This year I'm going to enter a 10K race.*

He ran two or three times per week, gradually increasing from his initial feat of running one block on March 15 to running seven miles (ten kilometers) in June without stopping to walk or to vomit. *I'm ready for the 10K,* he thought. How wrong he was. The day of the event, Stewart proudly wore his event T-shirt, size large. He wouldn't have fit into that size six months ago! At the sound of the cap gun, the runners were off. Now Stewart wasn't racing per se; his goal was just to run the 10K without stopping to walk. Around the fifth mile, Stew was doing great, enjoying the run, and he felt prematurely confident about finishing with his best time ever. But at mile six, he hit a wall. Every muscle screamed out for oxygen. His pace slackened, the sweat poured, and regrettably, he stopped.

Athletes often describe hitting a wall of performance. It is a barrier where no apparent amount of effort enables the athlete to push through the pain of the moment. Athletes who hit such a barrier surrender to it, as Stewart did, or they devise new understandings of the mind and disciplines of the body to help break through the barriers of their efforts.

Kurt liked his job when he first started out. The hours were good, his commute was reasonable, and the pay was standard for his entry-level position. But as time wore on, he became less and less enamored with his job. Cleaning bleachers after a pro baseball game suddenly seemed more appealing than the bean counting he did for eight hours a day, and if he ever had to do another month-end report, he thought he might expire right there on the spot. But he kept at it, working and working, day after day. After each evaluation he received a small raise, but it never provided much of a boost to his lagging vocational enthusiasm. Despite his growing discontent, Kurt simply refused to look for another job. There were better jobs available, closer to home, more stimulating for the mind, better beans to count—but the motivation simply wasn't there. For some reason, he continued working at the job he hated instead of investigating other options. He was, in a word, stuck.

Churches and church leaders face similar barriers. They hit a wall. They get stuck. Often, it is a barrier that exists because of repeated patterns of behavior. Lyle Schaller calls this "path dependency."[1] Once people and/or institutions travel down a certain path, it is difficult to choose a new road. Having gotten what we have always gotten, we continue to do what we have always done. How many times have we constrained ourselves to destructive patterns in the church that prevent our ability to experience God-sized ministry? Barriers to your ministry exist! Barriers are part of the human condition. Some of them you know about, others are perceptible, but still others hide under the surface and threaten to damage your ministry leadership. For effective ministry, you must identify, confront, and overcome these barriers.

> A *growth barrier* is a set of qualitative factors that create a ceiling to quantitative progress. A *leadership barrier* is a barrier that exists in

the mind, the heart, or the gift mix of the church leader.

Obviously, as I have been saying throughout this book, the number of people attending your church is not the only quantitative manner in which to evaluate your ministry impact. A God-sized ministry always seeks to produce personal, family, and community change to the glory of God. But several barriers have been observed in churches related to the number in attendance and the corresponding size plateaus. God-sized churches are aware of these barriers and successfully navigate the challenges they present for the leadership.

Lyle Schaller, Hartford Seminary, Leadership Network, and other researchers have suggested groupings of various size as a way to categorize church ministries. Here are sizes that I often use:

Figure 3
Church Size Categories Based on Attendance

Descriptor	Average Attendance
Very Small	0–99
Small	100–199
Medium	200–399
Large	400–799
Very Large	800–1,999
Mega	2,000+

These numerical barriers might not be experienced exactly as shown in the chart, but in most cases these barriers can be observed at the specific demarcations. Of all these barriers, the two hundred barrier is the most notable in that 85 percent of churches in North America stay below it. The dynamics that relate to this barrier are mostly predictable, and from a leadership perspective it marks the quantitative divide between small churches and large churches. Every size grouping of church has unique factors and makeup (referred to here as its DNA). Each size grouping also has its own size constraints. In the next few chapters I will provide insight into the most commonly referenced growth barriers. In my work with church leaders, I have observed an additional six barriers. These barriers are not primarily numeric; they are leadership barriers of mind, heart, and teamwork:

1. The barrier of *vision*—a breakthrough of **clarity**
2. The barrier of *leadership*—a breakthrough of **certainty**
3. The barrier of *team*—a breakthrough of **unity**
4. The barrier of *community*—a breakthrough of **connection**
5. The barrier of *presentation*—a breakthrough of **excellence**
6. The barrier of *follow-through*—a breakthrough of **faithfulness**

Each represents a qualitative leadership barrier to a God-sized ministry. In the next two chapters, we will examine these leadership barriers—and how to break through them—before we tackle the numerical barriers.

11.

Leadership Barriers, Part 1

In the course of these next two chapters, we will look at six specific leadership barriers to God-sizing your church. I am indebted to Carl George and Warren Bird for introducing these categories in their excellent book *How to Break Growth Barriers*. It is my goal, by examining each of these leadership barriers in light of the mission to God-size your church, to equip you in your leadership role, no matter what the current size of your organization. Then the following chapters will equip you regarding specific size barriers and how you can lead through them. The first three leadership barriers (addressed in this chapter as "Part 1") relate to your personal worldview and the relationships on your team. The latter three (addressed in chapter 12 as "Part 2") address the way that your ministry conducts itself in your community.

Barrier #1: The Barrier of Vision: A Breakthrough of Clarity

Cindi has been a committed volunteer at her church for the past five years. In fact, she tends to be a favorite around the church office with her uncompromising work ethic and ability to make things happen. Cindi is a model lay leader in many respects: hardworking, supportive of the church's mission and direction, and outreach oriented. She directs the early childhood education at the church, coordinates some outreach sports teams, and occasionally plays flute with the praise team.

After a challenging Christmas season, Cindi makes some changes to her priorities and scheduling to better balance family and ministry demands. But no matter what she does, she cannot come up with a creative solution to the problems that have been plaguing early childhood ministries for the last eight months. The elementary-age ministry is thriving and creating unique solutions to the issues facing it on a weekly basis, but in the early childhood classes, Cindi feels that she is continually banging her head against the wall. How should the department cope with the space issues, the increase in attendance throughout the weeks, and the multiple problems that success in church ministry causes? No matter how hard she works, the solutions remain elusive. She is stymied. She loves the challenges but wants more solutions.

What Cindi and many church leaders seek is clarity. The reality of day-to-day ministry in the trenches—outreach, equipping, education, counsel, and crises—creates multiple demands for church leaders on a regular basis. If the church at large is unclear on the ultimate goals and objectives of the local church ministry, the church will not reach those goals corporately. Likewise, if Cindi doesn't start to work together with her team to find creative solutions to the problems plaguing her ministry, it will plateau and decline over time. She needs what all of us need: a clear vision for her subministry, flowing directly from the church vision that can help her move in the right direction. Harder work will get things done, but it won't automatically lead to accomplishing the vision. The ministry requires the breakthrough of clarity.

If it is true that everything rises and falls on the issue of leadership, it is also true that the leadership in place must have a clear vision of where it is going. Obviously, if you do not know where you are going, you will never know when you get there!

Vision starts with you. Many teenagers struggle during these difficult transition years as they wrestle with the question, "Why am I here?" But this wrestling match is not just reserved for teens! Many adults wrestle with this million-dollar question as well—finding our purpose on this earth is critical to our ability to find a "zone" of ministry and impact lives forever. Clear vision starts with the question, "Why did God create me and put me in this place at this time?" As you search and find that answer, you will also find more clarity in how your own leadership impacts the vision of your church or ministry organization.

Clarity of vision must answer the question, "For whom does my church exist?"

Leaders of God-sized churches know who they are, why they are, and where they are. They have learned to operate out of their strengths and to mitigate their weaknesses. They know their key role and how to parlay that role into motivated ministry. Leaders of God-sized churches know where they are going and build bridges to the future while they are walking there.

Barrier #2: The Barrier of Leadership: A Breakthrough of Certainty

Pastor Jerry looked around the conference room at the members of his staff—all five of them. The associate pastor of the last two years was performing above average and led the community care ministries. The youth pastor often looked tired, but things were going fine with the youth and no one's car had been broken into for ten months, a new church record. The secretary/communications director was doing her work duties well enough, but she didn't support Jerry's leadership the way he hoped a key support staffer would and she was divisive in the office. The outreach director (still a volunteer position) was doing his job acceptably, but he had worked for a lengthier time under the previous senior pastor and continued to espouse the former leader's position on various issues. Fifth was the worship leader, who continued to butt heads with Jerry—not about the type of music, but about the length of the worship set within the service.

The church was poised to have a huge positive impact on the community of 180,000. There had been rumblings about great things going on at the church, which had a prime location. When the fifteen acres next door were donated to the church, the transaction made headlines on the front page of the city paper. They had a great buzz in the community, a great location, great potential. Yet as Jerry looked around the room, he realized that in the midst of all the greatness, he had a mediocre team. He left the meeting, went into his church study, and decided to do something about it.

Jerry was continually frustrated with a so-so staff that lacked passion and energy in a community searching for answers and looking to the church for some of those answers. In a rash attempt for a quick fix, he called Don, a mentor three hours away, and asked for—gasp—help! *He won't have time to help me*, Jerry thought as he dialed the number. *He's probably not even receiving calls today.* But in a serendipitous moment, the secretary patched him directly through, and Don sounded happy to hear his voice. As luck would have it (read: God), Don was to be in the area in two weeks, and they arranged to have a long lunch while they discussed strategy.

During the lunch, Jerry came to several revelations: the church income wasn't a big problem at the moment, but his staff configuration was. He had several options open to him, but remember, he didn't realize that his team was the biggest problem until two weeks earlier.

- The associate was gifted, but almost all of the gifts were in Jerry's areas of expertise. The care groups were hobbling along, but the associate's passions were in the areas of teaching and exposition—and he had the gift of leadership like Jerry did. The solution: put his leadership and teaching gifts to good use in a young adult/young family outreach-style ministry outside of Sunday morning. It took off like a rocket, and the associate essentially served as pastor of that subcongregation, which thrived under his leadership.
- The outreach pastor had good ideas, but he was stuck in the past. Jerry had lunch with him and explained some strains in the team as they related to the outreach position. The staffer accepted the pastor's critique, he formed an outreach team that included lay leaders, and they took on visitor follow-up with passion and excellence.
- Jerry discussed the worship possibilities with Don and came up with creative solutions to the children's ministry problems that were preventing the adults from adding ten minutes to their service. Doing that eased the worship leader's frustration and gave the whole congregation what they really wanted in the first place—more time to worship.
- There was some flexibility with staffing since the children's director had recently moved and the position was vacant. For some time Jerry wanted to move a key lay leader into a staff position, but the communications director in the office was tying up resources that could have been better used. He met with the communications director, discussed the

staffing changes, and gave her two months to find another job. She found another job in five days and quit early. This change allowed Jerry to bring the key lay leader onto the staff into the children's director role and make the communications role a lay-led position.

- Jerry brought in training resources for the youth staffer to help him build a stronger team of volunteers so that most of the work didn't fall on his shoulders.

Pastoral leaders with a clear vision understand the importance of aligning gifts and passion with the purposes of the church. Developing a winning team means the senior leader surrounds himself or herself with people who have complementary gifts, buy in to the vision of the ministry, and are willing to work in a team environment. Michael Jordan is an unequaled basketball player not only because of his individual talents (which are *huge*) but also because of his ability to bring out each team member's talent.

All the time that Pastor Jerry thought the problem was with other elements of the ministry, the problem was with his own leadership! He had lacked the certainty to make difficult but necessary changes to the church staff and structure. Bold, confident leadership was required, and when Jerry stepped up to that task, the solutions became clear. Remember, ministry is war. Paul reminds us that our struggle is not against flesh and blood, but it is nonetheless a struggle, a war. You are in a foxhole with a team of people who will advance the cause, fail morally and lose ground, or tread in the waters of mediocrity. The barrier of certainty is a difficult barrier to face, but the success of your leadership depends on your willingness to boldly take responsibility for the mission.

Barrier #3: The Barrier of Team: A Breakthrough of Unity

Doug and Lisa were in love at first sight—almost. Doug had been interested in Lisa ever since they met at the college group's all-night party at the nearby amusement park. But since Doug accidentally spilled his hot coffee all over Lisa's back while they were in line for the big roller coaster, it took a few weeks for Lisa to become interested in Doug!

Doug was a gifted teacher in the adult small-group ministry at the church. He wasn't called by God into vocational ministry, but his church taught spiritual gifts well enough that he recognized his gifts and enjoyed using them in ministry. Lisa (after recovering from the coffee incident) also became committed to ministry at the church. Although she had spent a few years bouncing from ministry area to ministry area, she ultimately caught a vision for the fifth and sixth grade department and went wild there. It was a perfect fit: the kids loved her energy, her passion for God, and her relevance, and she loved helping shape the kids' values before they faced the pressures of middle school. During their engagement and subsequent marriage, Doug and Lisa led the young adult small group at the church, and Lisa team-taught the fifth and sixth grade Sunday school class.

Pastor Jim loved Doug and Lisa. He hadn't personally led them to Christ, but from the day he started at the church, he knew that they were a dynamic, influential couple who were, in his words, "keepers." Not only was their love for God evident in what they did, but their commitment to invest in the lives of others shone through their weekly ministry projects. They were a delight to have at the church, and every year they seemed to be more and more effective.

About six years after their wedding, which Jim performed, he asked Doug out to lunch and challenged him to serve on the church leadership team. Their church had a one-board leadership structure, and being asked to serve was a privilege usually given to people in their thirties and older. Jim didn't want Doug's age at that time (twenty-eight) to be a barrier for him, and Doug said yes. The other board members were pleased with Doug's and Lisa's track records and heartily welcomed him to the board. His nomination and vote were unchallenged.

It wasn't long, though, before Doug started dreading the meetings. They were not openly contentious by any means, and no one received a black eye. But there was something he couldn't put his finger on—something that distressed him. He served three years on the board and continued to teach Bible studies—and Lisa took over the fifth and sixth grade ministry and grew it well. Soon forty preteens were coming to their midweek ministry night!

The more Doug worked alongside other leaders in problem solving, the more he realized that a group at the church didn't support Jim's pastorate. It wasn't that they disliked him personally (although a few did); they didn't support the vision. It was getting worse—not better—and really ate at Doug's stomach every time the board met.

Over lunch one afternoon, Doug and Pastor Jim openly discussed the issue. It turned out that things were worse than Doug knew. A faction group on the board asked Jim to resign, and an entire adult Sunday school class wrote him a letter to that effect. They knew "what they wanted in a church," and they knew Jim "was not the man to lead it," the letter read. Jim had been looking for other work, but he didn't feel released from his ministry assignment yet, so he clung to it with patience despite the opposition.

From there, things got even worse. The contentious group started calling Doug at work and at home, telling him things about the church. Doug couldn't discern whether they were true, false, or a little of both. The stressors in the church were weighing on Lisa's heart, and her ministry with the preteens was suffering. Furthermore, Lisa's students were picking up information from different sources, and that caused them to ask questions about churches and pastors that she was simply unprepared to answer. Life was hard, and it wasn't getting easier. Doug internalized a lot of his anger and hopelessness, and ultimately developed an ulcer.

The strain of ministry conflict was getting worse, and Doug's health was not good. When his doctor asked him if he needed a medical leave from his job for a week, Doug realized that what he really needed was medical leave from his church. In the midst of a strained and difficult ministry environment at a church Doug and Lisa loved, they began the heartrending decision process of whether to leave.

They knew that they couldn't let Doug's health be the primary issue because he needed to respond differently to the conflict and not internalize it and then blame the church for his ulcers. But over time it became clear to them that they couldn't continue to minister effectively in a church where ugliness and meanness increasingly won out over love and reconciliation. After twelve months of soul-searching and many nights of tears, Doug and Lisa left the church.

Larry Osborne, pastor of North Coast Community Church in the San Diego area, has written *The Unity Factor*. While it is a small book, it has a powerful message: "Get the key influencers in your church to share a common vision. Sacrifice today for the promise of tomorrow in these people's lives."[1] Without leadership unity, there will be no lasting ministry growth that breaks through barriers.

My friend Don Nelson is a committed lay leader in a church that has worked with several church plants to help them launch well. He sent me a note in 2001 describing the divisiveness in his church:

> At our church, my wife and I are giving time we don't have, and tons of money because it's important. Do you think we are going to let sick people kill that work and investment? Heavens no! It's costing us way too much! For every sick, agenda laden, divisive, contentious person in our church we aren't willing to confront (out of fear, we say "oh that's just the way they are," or "I don't think God wants us to treat people like that," etc.), there are 10, 20, 100, 1000 people out there to be won to Christ that won't because they sniff out the contentiousness and will go somewhere else. Do we want to stand before God and say we did the math wrong, or that we didn't have the guts to make way for hundreds more to come to Christ by not tackling these problems decisively?

We planted Carson Valley Christian Center with ten core values in mind. One of these values states our intention to address conflict and contentiousness head-on: "Core Value 4: Community life in the church family is so honored that division and gossip are confronted quickly and clearly, and resolved in accordance with biblical principles of fellowship and conflict resolution."

Matthew 18:15-17 discusses specifically what we are to do if a believer sins against us and how we are to go about reconciliation. It is critically important that we face conflict and its related issues head-on so that the mess of unresolved issues does not fester and seethe:

"If your brother sins against you, go and show him his fault, just between the two of you. If he listens to you, you have won your brother over. But if he will not listen, take one or two others along, so that 'every matter may be established by the testimony of two or three witnesses.' If he refuses to listen to them, tell it to the church; and if he refuses to listen even to the church, treat him as you would a pagan or a tax collector."

A God-sized church must have its core leadership unified in the vision, in harmony with one another, and committed together in the focus on ministry to the community. Larry Osborne's book *The Unity Factor* makes clear that churches that push forward with programs, activities, and structure without unity do so at their peril. Countless stories of church division and difficulty can be told about churches that never arrived at unity of purpose and vision. A growing church will be led by a leader who understands the imperative of developing unity and cohesiveness among the key leaders.

A growing church must also be clear about the call to maturity. When believers are constantly bickering, creating a climate of backbiting and division, the potential for effective kingdom ministry is virtually nonexistent. Leaders must model and exhort their congregations toward spiritual maturity and present visible patterns of conflict resolution that engender authentic community within the family. Tragically, many churches have chosen the path of least resistance rather than the avenue of greatest spiritual impact. Unity must be present to break through growth barriers.

Some churches are so conflicted and contentious that a long-term solution is far from reach. But in many cases the church has simply failed to teach and practice the

Matthew 18 principles of conflict resolution and the sin-forgiveness process. In some churches, resolving conflict is not a core value. What could happen in the kingdom of God if more churches decided to face sin and conflict in a godly manner?

12.

Leadership Barriers, Part 2

In the previous chapter, we reviewed three leadership barriers that relate primarily to the worldview of the leader and the team around that leader. In this chapter, the next three leadership barriers relate to the context of the community in which you serve. Former Senator Tip O'Neill wrote *All Politics Is Local* in 1993 to describe the reality that all politics come down to personal impact. Likewise, all ministry is local. Great plans, great strategies, great dreams ultimately all come down to the power of God to change a human heart. Until we see transformation in human life, we have not succeeded in experiencing what a God-sized vision for ministry is all about. These next three barriers will help you understand that in clear detail.

Barrier #4: The Barrier of Community: A Breakthrough of Connection

Pastor Dave sat at the deacon meeting listening to the latest report from the food pantry coordinator, but his mind was somewhere else. He was daydreaming about what their church was like five years ago. Then the church was bursting at the seams. Momentum was on their side. Young families were joining the church at record speed, and mature adults were reaching out to the community in strategic ways. Dave remembered reporting one year that the two hundred people who joined the church in the previous two years represented all the age brackets equally! People of all ages were coming in to the church and making commitments to Christ and to membership. Their church was truly intergenerational, and everyone loved it.

The mission team did a study of the church's local community of six hundred thousand and learned of strategic needs that county social services knew about but that were not yet funded. New need-based ministries were started and they thrived. Young families learned the importance of a Christ-centered marriage and family, and children were taught the gospel from an early age. The church was buzzing with activity, and you could feel the energy on a Sunday morning when you walked around.

Unfortunately, Pastor Dave snapped out of his daydream and wondered what had gone wrong. In actuality, nothing had gone wrong. The church was still poised for influence, but it was poised to affect a different community—for theirs had changed right under their noses. Both of the air force bases within thirty-five miles had closed in the last five years, and only a small percentage of the workforce remained behind as the bases transitioned to civilian industries. Furthermore, four years ago a brand-new retirement village was built in a small community forty-five miles south of the church. Positioned on three golf courses, this housing behemoth (with houses, apartments, partial-care and total-care facilities) was becoming famous in the tricounty area and was attracting a huge number of mature adults from the surrounding communities. Many young families liked the school district in that southern suburb and moved as well. Six months previously, that community incorporated and became its own municipality.

All in all, Dave could list 176 people who had left his church because the base closures meant they had to find work elsewhere or because they moved to the sprawling community to the south. And that didn't count the stream of people who would have been potential members from the air force. However, their steady stream of visitors was still in place. It was the visitors themselves who were different! The city was not dwindling by any means. Even though some industries were moving out, several new large companies were relocating there. The population had actually gown substantially in the last year, and the church could have a dramatic impact if it understood the new community that had developed around it. How would the church thrive and grow in the next five years? What should church members and leaders do?

Some members and even leaders of churches do not have the first clue about the communities in which they live, work, and serve. Sometimes the reason is that they live in a Christian bubble, seldom interacting with the unchurched around them. But other times this cluelessness stems from a lack of homework. To know your community, you must study it. Who lives near your church? For example, imagine that your ministry is located in a community where the average annual household income (an easily obtained figure) is $80,000, and one in six households has an income that exceeds $140,000. How would your outreach focus be different from that of a church located in the heart of a college community with thousands of single people? The heart of the gospel would never change, but the way that you advertise, the way that you perform music, and the style of speaking would be vastly different.

God-sized churches break through growth barriers because they are effective students of their community culture. If the local McDonald's owner knows more about your community than you do as a pastor, your church is in trouble. Breaking through growth barriers means you understand how to reach your community. Robert Schuller said it best when he proclaimed that churches must "find a need and fill it, find a hurt and heal it."[1] Barrier-busting ministry always finds a way to connect with the community and meet needs in the name of Christ.

A friend of mine pastors a church in a changing area. Previously, the workforce commuted to towns up to an hour away. That meant workers got home late at night and had difficulty participating in midweek activities. Now, the workforce has shifted (due to business relocations), and people work closer to home. While people can now work in the same town where they live and worship, the community is more fast-paced and heterogeneous. The frenzy of city life—from which their little town had been a getaway—reached their neighborhood.

Changes in the workforce produced dramatic changes in the community. People who were once wrapped up in their commute time now live in the midst of their workplaces. The nature of what their community means to them changed. Family activities shifted, and school security concerns heightened. A sleepy little town became a bustling city. My friend's church now offers a menu of parent and family activities centered on neighborhoods, providing learning and connecting opportunities for strangers to become friends in safe places. All the while, the ministry of 95 percent of the churches in the area has not changed in two decades. The implications of social change for ministry are *huge*, but too few churches recognize the needs or opportunities when they present themselves.

Jesus, the master teacher, laced His teaching with metaphors and illustrations that the crowds would understand. It's a basic tenet of Christianity, but one that is often overlooked. Because the gospel and so many central truths will never change, churches tend to do the same things the same way as well. And suddenly, after forty years of the same things, they realize that their community has changed completely from what it was, and the church has lost touch. When the church remains the same while the community changes, the church almost always declines. And a declining church is giving up ground in the war for people's souls.

Barrier #5: The Barrier of Presentation: A Breakthrough of Excellence

Bill was the drama director at First Baptist Church. He did his ministry well, and usually once a month the drama department at the church helped illustrate the pastor's teaching with a humorous and relevant sketch. The congregation loved it, and even attendees of the traditional service—at first skeptical of the idea—grew to love these "slice of life" illustrations.

Pastor Sam was thrilled with how the drama ministry was shaping the teaching and vice versa. He watched his congregation's eyes light up each time there was a drama, and he knew that if the drama team could pull together something longer for Christmas weekend, their ability to make an impression on their people and the visitors they brought would be huge. He set Bill to work, and a twenty-minute modern-day Christmas drama was developed.

After the show was cast, the team went to work blocking and memorizing the piece. All, it seemed, except Steve. Steve was a member of the church who worked at the local grocery store as the assistant manager. His hours were long, but fortunately, he had a consistent schedule and could make all the rehearsals. Tuesday nights weren't the problem—but his attitude was. The deadline to be off book, to have all the lines memorized, was November 15. But Thanksgiving came and went, and Steve hadn't learned his part. When other drama team members teased him about it after the rehearsal on December 10, he said something about its being "only for church" and got in his car. One member remarked, "Only for church? What does that mean?"

Five days before the production, Steve still didn't know all his lines, and although he wasn't playing the main role, his character was central to the production and several key lines depended on his dialogue and timing being precise. Bill, the director, had never tried to pull off a twenty-minute drama in key holiday services, and they were about to do two within two weeks, and his blood was boiling. Pastor Sam came to observe a rehearsal a week before the Christmas weekend and left sullen. The show was not coming together, and Steve was the problem. When Bill and Steve met the next night, Steve talked about how he would memorize his part "when the time came" and not to worry. "Besides," he said again and again, "it's only for church. It's not a big deal. It's not like we're getting paid to get this job done. It'll work out fine."

Unfortunately, Steve's attitude is pervasive in the church. Unchurched people have come to expect (but not accept!) mediocrity whenever they do attend church. Even worse, churchgoers have come to expect and accept mediocrity from others as well as themselves when it comes to presentation-oriented ministry. Few people have the guts to stand up and say, "This is bad. God is not pleased with us offering the leftovers of what we could offer Him." God is pleased with sacrifice, with excellence, with our best. Consider this warning from Malachi: " 'When you bring blind animals for sacrifice, is that not wrong? When you sacrifice crippled or diseased animals, is that not wrong? Try offering them to your governor! Would he be pleased with you? Would he accept you?' says the LORD Almighty" (Malachi 1:8).

Sometimes the attitude expressed by Steve is held not only by lay leaders but also by the staff! If that is true in your church, then the road ahead for you is long and hard. If your staff accepts mediocrity because key players are unwilling or unable to expect better, then those players must be retrained or replaced. You cannot accept a mediocre staff any more than you can afford to accept a mediocre presentation each weekend.

Excellence in your weekend service presentation is critical to your success in taking new ground for the kingdom. I believe most churches need to narrow their targets of excellence. For most churches today, these three excellence targets are essential for weekend services:

1. Excellence in weekend teaching
2. Excellence in worship and musical presentation
3. Excellence in children's ministries

When Carson Valley Christian Center was planted and launched in February 1998, we decided to attain excellence in these areas from day one. People are attracted to and stay at a church because of excellence in one or more of these top three areas; they simply must have the utmost priority for your entire fellowship. Sometimes the dark question that few churches have the guts to ask their people is this: "Would you be more likely to invite your unchurched friends and neighbors to our church if the presentation in one or more of the top three areas were improved? Does our mediocrity prevent you from inviting anyone to our church?"

We live in a time where *ought* doesn't cut it anymore. Telling someone that she ought to come to church won't budge her from her notions of irrelevance. But presenting a warm, excellent worship service that touches the heart, stimulates the mind, and engages the soul will break through the barriers of heart resistance. Paying attention to specific ministry needs (children's ministry, first impressions ministry, and age-graded programming) with excellence demonstrates commitment to your vision of reaching people.

Sometimes churches fail to offer an excellent, well-rounded presentation on the weekends because the church is trying to do more than it can do well. Obviously, the goal would be to do everything well. But I challenge you first to do fewer things well rather than more things poorly. Then work up to more and more as you conquer the challenging areas with assertiveness and excellence.

Barrier #6: The Barrier of Follow-through: A Breakthrough of Faithfulness

Susan recently became the volunteer assimilation coordinator of her local church. The pastor asked her to find out what had happened over the course of the past three years. Many people had visited St. Peter's during that period, but few had stayed. Also, some people who had been relatively longtime attendees had started to diminish their involvement, and Pastor George was afraid that meant something he couldn't quite figure out.

Susan developed a team of five people who began systematically calling visitors who had not stayed at St. Peter's. Over time, they discovered a pattern that shocked them. Even though St. Peter's had always considered itself a friendly church, many visitors shared a similar story. The official greeters warmly greeted them at the door. However, in each and every case, no other person spoke to them. The visitors left feeling that St. Peter's was not really a warm and friendly place.

After about fifteen calls with similar results, Susan presented her results to her pastor. In the meantime, George had spoken to several of the longtime attendees who appeared to be detaching from the church. As it turned out, they had a somewhat similar experience. Many of those who were lessening their involvement at St. Peter's told a story about feeling that they "no longer fit" and they were not "insiders" anymore but increasingly felt like "outsiders." After prayer and conversation, George and Susan concluded that St. Peter's had a problem with cliques, and that simply could not continue if the church was to be healthy.

The Apostle Paul wrote, "Let us not become weary in doing good, for at the proper time we will reap a harvest if we do not give up" (Galatians 6:9). Paul had it tough: he traveled around as an itinerant missionary, planting churches right and left. He had to leave those churches in (sometimes) trustworthy hands, and then he had to sit in jail and hear horror stories about how bad things got and (in at least one case) how a man sleeping with his stepmother was affirmed and accepted by a church that Paul shepherded and loved. How much worse could it get? Paul apparently knew what he was doing when he wrote, inspired by the Holy Spirit, for us not to grow weary, not to give up. Perhaps Paul needed that truth for himself as much as the Galatians did, and one can picture him weeping (or possibly banging his head against his cell wall) as he dictated that sentence. Ministry is hard work. Not giving up—that is even harder.

Winston Churchill gave a famous and oft-quoted speech in which he stated, "Never give in, never give in, never, never, never, never." Sometimes in ministry that is all we need to hear. Another often-repeated quotation that has entered "churchianity" culture is this one: "God is not interested in your ability, but in your availability." Obviously, God prepared in advance for us to do good works (Ephesians 2:10) so it is not fair to say that our abilities are not of concern to God. But the point is well taken—that daily yielding our hearts to our Father and His Son is of utmost concern to Him, and that miraculous things happen in our lives and in the lives of those we influence when we choose to make ourselves available to God. During World War II, Corrie Ten Boom was a young woman who felt called by God to save Jewish people through an underground set up in her home. She prayed a similar prayer one dark night in occupied Holland: "Lord Jesus, I offer myself for Your people. In any way. Any place. Any time."[2] God used Corrie in some amazing ways that she previously never thought possible as she ministered to hundreds, if not thousands, in her hometown of Haarlem and in the concentration camp where she eventually was imprisoned.

God, by the power of His spirit, is able to sustain us through hardships we never thought were possible to survive, with our faith intact. He is able to comfort us, give us peace, and strengthen us during the dark moments. Corrie Ten Boom experienced this when she and her sister were thrown into a concentration camp. But repeatedly, Scripture challenges us to persevere, to hold on, to run the race, to triumph. So in Scripture we find a both/and phenomenon surrounding the reality of perseverance: that there are sustaining factors through the Spirit, and there are choices to be made by us as individuals. Both are in the equation, and both are necessary not to grow "weary in doing good."

Once you know the right thing for your vision, your leadership, your community, just do it! Do it again and again. Do it well. Do it right. Do it consistently and faithfully. Persistent execution of your vision will produce a harvest. Practice continuous improvement, and be a laser beam rather than a shotgun. A shotgun approach is usually tempting to us since it makes a lot of noise and produces an immediate response from our people. But the laser beam approach will be quieter and more exacting, and will yield results worth waiting for: a harvest!

It has been my experience that staying the course relates to four specific dimensions; each of them requires constant attention and poses strategic questions:

1. *Call:* Are you clear about God's call on your life, your call to ministry, and the vision He has for you and for those you shepherd?
2. *Character:* What are the essentials of heart and mind that make up the "you" that you want to be? What is the epitaph you want written on your tombstone by your family, friends, *and* your adversaries? Are you clear about how your character has been shaped and is shared with others?
3. *Community:* Do you have anchor relationships in your life? Are there people into whom you have invested and who keep you accountable and can undergird your life during a storm? All ministry flows out of relationships. Are you building a community of relationships that model and contribute health in your life?
4. *Competency:* Have you identified your gifts? Are you continuously improving your kingdom effectiveness with your gifts?

Perseverance in ministry always relates to clarity of vision *and* persistence in follow-through. In short, knowing what to do and doing it consistently well are key! Basically, there are two ways to grow a church: "We must bring people in the front door, and we must keep people from going out the 'back door.' "[3] This process takes time, energy, and more effort than you will have on some days. But never give up. In time you will reap a harvest, and God will give you wisdom and direction as you seek to bring in people and to keep people from leaving for the wrong reasons.

13.

Frying Pan Size 1: Under 200

The average church in America has seventy-five participants in worship on Sunday morning, according to the National Congregations Study from Hartford Seminary.[1] Approximately 94 percent of churches in America have fewer than five hundred people in worship each week, according to the same study. In this chapter, we will examine the specific leadership challenges for those leading congregations with fewer than two hundred people in weekend worship.

Virtually all the issues relate to how the pastor and the people interact about the role of the pastor. If you are a pastor of this size church, you will recognize many issues addressed here, such as expectations of leadership and ways to grow existing leaders and emerge new worldviews.

My prayer is that you will hear a fresh call from God about how to help you and your dear people become part of God's plan to reach more for Christ in your community.

In light of the large number of small churches in the United States, one might think that perhaps people have chosen to cluster in small churches because of specific benefits, including these:

- intimate and tightly knit community
- small-town feel: easy to know what others are doing and what they are learning
- spiritually close relationships

Some churches are small because their communities are small or declining in population. Over time cities and towns change, and in many parts of the country, the small community is the norm and not the exception. When the number of people is small because of external factors, including the reality of social change (for example, declining population, aging population, economic disruption), the challenge is to make the church a healthy and wholesome environment for maximizing spiritual growth. Several useful resources are available for those leading smaller congregations to health, such as the *Ministry in the Small Membership Church* series by Abingdon Press and additional resources at www.easum bandy.com and www.alban.org.

For many churches, however, the two hundred barrier is unrelated to the size of the community or to economic or social issues. Many small churches are intentionally small for social reasons, not spiritual reasons. I would challenge those of us who lead small churches to carefully determine whether external factors have kept our churches small or (as I suspect) we have made the intentional choice not to reach more people for personal and social reasons. We do not find biblical mandates for small churches anywhere in Scripture, and time and time again believers are charged with the task of unending outreach. Sadly, some small churches are small because the members want it that way, regardless of the biblical imperative for outreach.

Furthermore, in most small churches the staff and lay leaders perform so many tasks that many of those tasks fall outside their primary and secondary spiritual gifts. The net result is a group of believers serving in ministry roles where they are not equipped to serve, leading to frustration, mediocrity, and eventual burnout. If you look closely at a warm, tightly knit small church, you will find a lot of tired leaders doing ministry in areas they do not enjoy, performing tasks they are not meant to do. Pastors and leaders of these churches must cooperatively learn to focus their energies and efforts on what will best enable them to fulfill the Great Commission.

The two hundred barrier is caused by several converging factors listed below. Some factors are easy to identify and correct.

Congregation Mind-set

A small congregation, for the most part, has a small mind-set and might even hold small as a spiritual value. Many think that larger churches are not godly because if they are attractive to many people, they must not hold high standards. Crowd drawing then becomes a secular success instead of strategic ministry. To the contrary, many people attend larger churches because the service is done with excellence and laypeople can serve in their areas of giftedness and experience.

Many small-church attendees enjoy the fact that they all know and love one another, and they hold tightly to their right to vote on everything. A more difficult issue to pinpoint is the struggle with the sin of pride by some small-church congregants. Some people have a strong need to be known and loved, and they cannot get that attention and status in a larger church. Sometimes without even realizing it, churchgoers in a small church will thwart every attempt to grow the church because of their self-satisfying interests and their need to be noticed. This "big fish in the small pond" disease is death to a growing church and must be confronted and eliminated, and the biblical mandate for evangelism must be explicitly taught.

Leadership Qualities and Choices

Many pastors of churches with fewer than two hundred people attending weekend worship tend to make choices to herd sheep instead of herding shepherds (also known as sheep ranchers). Those serving in these roles must accept the responsibility to provide excellent *systems* of care rather than the personal (and impossible!) burden of providing all the care. Although some choices are based directly on the congregation's expectations to be pastored directly by the pastor whenever they need her, at other times these choices reflect what the pastor expects from her leadership.

Pastors are tasked to equip the saints for the work of the ministry (Ephesians 4). Many pastors choose to overburden—and thus, limit—themselves by doing all the tasks of ministry rather than equipping others to minister in their areas of giftedness. One specific task that most pastors should not be doing is pastoral counseling. If pastors are truly to be equippers for ministry, most senior pastors should stop counseling everyone and set up lay leadership to handle much of the counseling load. How much more impact could the church have for the kingdom if people received counsel from someone who had the spiritual gift of discernment instead of the senior pastor who might not possess this gift in counseling situations?

Pastors of smaller churches also continually fall into the manager's trap, that is, most of the time the leader is micromanaging different ministries instead of letting go of the leadership reins and releasing ministry. Small failures will inevitably happen with this strategy, but major successes will be won when people are mobilized and receive the call to do ministry in the trenches. Consider the behaviors of sheepherders, who limit the size of a flock, as contrasted with the behaviors of sheep ranchers, who understand how to release ministry into the hands of others:

Sheepherders
- personally do *all* the caring
- attempt to meet *all* expectations
- work to the limit of their time and energy
- keep work close to themselves
- base perspective on present conditions

Sheep ranchers
- ensure high-quality pastoral care
- set expectations for others
- perceive the church organizationally
- delegate and involve others
- develop leadership and management skills

Church Polity and Infrastructure

The very organization and structuring of small churches are often barriers to their growth. In many small churches, people hold on to their right to vote as if their salvation itself were at stake. There are several concerns with this approach. First of all, too many church-goers lack the biblical knowledge, understanding of truth, and fortitude in the evangelical mandate to direct a church in keeping with a strategic vision. Second, you simply cannot lead a church by committee. If it is really difficult to plan a large party with a committee full of people with different ideas and agendas, then why do we expect a church to be led well by scores of committees? Each church should develop a small team of gifted leaders who have passion for the ministry and can help lead the church family.

Furthermore, smaller churches do not have the infrastructure to add any people to the system, and if more people were added, many systems would collapse. A helpful exercise for your ministry setting would be to list your weekend service attendance in every area of your ministry (large-group service, children's classrooms, adult classrooms, etc.). Now, add two hundred people to the system—or double the number of every single group in every room. Is there capacity? Is there enough adult supervision? Are there enough chairs?

Consider these three classifications of church infrastructure: relational, ministry, and leadership.

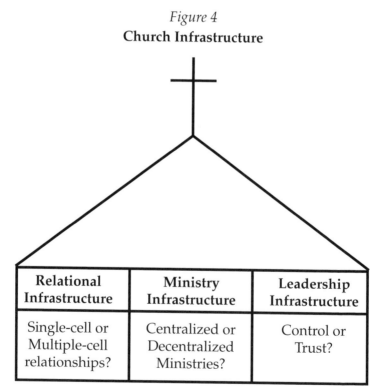

Figure 4
Church Infrastructure

Relational Infrastructure	Ministry Infrastructure	Leadership Infrastructure
Single-cell or Multiple-cell relationships?	Centralized or Decentralized Ministries?	Control or Trust?

These three categories of infrastructure affect the church at its fundamental core by creating barriers in the following ways:

1. Single-cell vs. multiple-cell relationships. Many small churches are made of single-cell groups that relate to the pastor of the church. Larger churches over the two hundred barrier have multiple cells of people groupings that interrelate with each other and the leadership of the church.
2. Centralized vs. decentralized ministries. Ministry over the two hundred barrier takes place in a decentralized fashion with ministries being delegated with trust.
3. Control vs. trust paradigm. Smaller churches tend to favor control over trust, while larger churches favor trust over control.

Developing Barrier-breaking Strategies

Author and church leader Bill Sullivan, in his book *New Perspectives on Breaking the 200 Barrier*, has developed a ten-step strategy that will help you break through the two hundred barrier:

1. Examine your motive: why do you want to stay where you are? Do you want to grow?
2. Intensify your praying: have you been praying for growth?
3. Increase your faith: believe that God can and will grow your fellowship.
4. Set a barrier-breaking goal: write down on paper a specific numeric goal.
5. Think through your plan: what are its strengths? What are its weaknesses? Show your plan to a large-church pastor for feedback and insight.

6. Focus on the critical few: which leaders under you are critical to the growth's success?
7. Create excitement: build momentum through testimonies, energy, hope.
8. Launch a growth thrust: be specific and strategic.
9. Evangelize first: focus on the biblical mandate to preach the gospel.
10. Lead the change: change things about your own leadership style and choices, and show by example that you are willing to change too.

Carl George and Warren Bird, in their book *How to Break Growth Barriers*, have also put together several ideas that will help you as you break through the two hundred barrier:

- Exude a contagious desire to grow: this flows from the top down.
- Articulate and enhance existing growth factors.
- Take next steps from sheepherder to rancher: start spending more of your time leading the leaders in your midst.
- Deal with institutional factors inhibiting growth: change issues that are preventing growth from happening.
- Resist returning to a small church mentality: do not cater to self-serving pew-warmers who only care about themselves.
- Establish a network of lay-led small groups: move the pastoral-care functions of the church into a small-group network where people can be known and loved by believers other than the pastor.

If you are the senior leader of a ministry seeking to break through the two hundred barrier, you must pick a pathway and go the distance to lead your people into God's vision for outreach in your community. As you God-size your church, you will see lives change for His glory!

14.

Frying Pan Size 2: 200–400

Of all the leadership challenges that pastors will face, this church size is perhaps the most difficult to lead. Recent research from Dave Olson of the Evangelical Covenant Church in America suggests that larger churches are growing because of their services and smaller churches are growing because of their intimacy.[1] Mid-sized churches then are faced with being unable to deliver either extreme. They are too big to be small, and they are too small to be big. Olson's research suggests that this size classification of church is declining. Based on my experience, breaking through the four hundred barrier involves leadership training, multiple entry points, and the pastor becoming a contractor rather than a carpenter. Allow me to explain.

Most pastors in America were trained as carpenters (or sheepherders as I described it in the previous chapter). What this means is that we understand hands-on ministry, working in direct contact with people. Once the church grows to somewhere between 150 and 200, it is humanly impossible for one person to keep up with the pastoral demands of the church congregation—which is why most churches are unable or unwilling to reach more than 150 to 200 people. In order to reach more people, the pastor and the people will have to come to agreement regarding the role of the pastor. Moving from being a carpenter to a contractor means the pastor will see his or her role from a management and organizational perspective, managing several carpenters rather than doing all the work himself or herself (using the construction analogy, it is the job of the contractor to manage the various subcontractor disciplines and provide what they need to complete their task). Invariably what results at this stage is a series of crises. I have provided a brief description of these crises and recommendations about how to navigate them.

Crisis of Identity

Churches between two hundred and four hundred in weekend attendance struggle more with identity than any other barrier. "Who are we now?" and "What were we then?" are typical questions that are continually asked. When the church was smaller, it felt as if everyone knew everyone else. (By the way, this was never true. However, since it is true in the mind of the speaker, to deny its reality is typically not helpful!). Now the church can often feel like a mass of people. This feeling is accentuated by having multiple services with related parking or space problems, and people feeling disconnected from any core identity as a church. I have encouraged pastors leading ministries emerging into this size to ensure that the mission/vision/values of the church are clear and consistently repeated across the contexts of ministry, and to ensure that healthy small-group environments exist for care and nurture.

There are two other helpful tools. First, honor the past history of the church. Those who grapple the most with feeling a loss of identity are typically those with historical roots in the church. Honor them by linking the current growth with the historical vision of the church. Second, provide at least a couple of events during the year where all church members can gather if they choose to do so (for example, outdoor picnics, combined worship celebration) and provide connections for your leadership core. Arranging for the leadership core of the church to gather at least twice annually will give increased ownership to the key stakeholders in the ministry.

Leadership Crisis

Recognizing the reality of church life at this stage often means a crisis in leadership. Not only must the senior leader no longer meet the totality of pastoral needs, but she must equip others to do much of the ministry that she previously did. Further, a leader at this size church must have the freedom to try new things and experiment with different ways to reach people. Most typically, the church has a leadership team combining paid and unpaid persons who will serve in staffing roles. My experience consulting with churches at this level indicates that the vast majority of leaders are ill-equipped to lead teams of people (see my book *Leveraging Your Leadership Style* for a basic primer on team leadership). Further, the senior leader at this level must embody the leadership maxim, "Speed of the leader, speed of the team." A leader who articulates values that he does not personally live out will soon find himself with questioning followers who doubt the heartbeat of the senior leader.

Multiple Service Crisis

The challenges of growth most often lead churches to offer additional services. The practical effect of holding at least two services is that it affords people multiple options to attend and to invite friends. In addition, it provides the opportunity to double the ministry servant workforce without requiring workers to miss worship. Churches that have at least two services are able to challenge people to serve on the weekends during a service hour without having to require a rotational system of missing worship services. All of this bodes well for offering multiple services whenever possible.

Even though more people are reached and involved, it again strikes at the heart of what many fear in a growing church. That is, in a church with multiple services, how will attendees ever see everyone together all at once? The simple and most direct answer is the most difficult: they won't. The painful truth is that a church reaching more people for Christ will have to make the decision that it will sacrifice the comfort level of having everyone at one place at one time (again, this never really happens, but it is the perception of people, so it is pointless to argue it) in order to God-size the ministry and reach and grow all those whom God has entrusted to the church. The crisis of multiple services is that it will require strategic leadership to ensure maximizing outreach, leadership, and facility capacities.

Crisis of Power

In my previous role as a denominational leader and now as a pastor/consultant, I have often talked with lay and pastoral church leaders about how their structure is either helping them to reach or hindering them from reaching their God-sized potential. This is usually not a pleasant experience (personally, I'd rather go to the dentist—no offense to dentists!). Amazingly, many people have a deeper commitment to the form of church government with which they have grown accustomed than to the missional function that governmental structure is to fulfill. I come from a Baptist background, and my experience is that church fights over church government are far more prevalent than church fights over doctrine and theology.

The way past this crisis of power always lies in a biblical vision for ministry. Pastoral leaders walking with their people through this season of change will need to help people find what is nonnegotiable in their experience with Christ and His church. In my leadership roles over the years, I have been able to assist people to recognize that the *how* we do something in church should always be subservient to the *why*. Once people grasp that concept, they can move toward changing the governmental structure to ensure the fulfillment of the vision rather than the continuity of the structure itself.

It was my great joy, while in my early twenties, to work with several long-term church members on the board of my second church. In that church, I learned a very valuable lesson that served me well in later denominational and consulting roles. Most people (yes, there are exceptions!) really want their church to succeed in reaching their community. When I was able to love people and teach them God's word with clarity and conviction, they allowed me to lead them well. God-sizing church leaders will cultivate a culture of passion for the Great Commission and Great Commandment while leading people to prioritize missional function over governmental form.

Change Crisis

Another leadership crisis in a church of this size has to do with the process of change. The human body has only a certain capacity for change (which is why our bodies can go into shock when there is too much loss of blood), as does any organizational system. For many of the crises discussed previously in this chapter, the root issue is change itself. Leaders who help their churches move past this growth barrier will learn to navigate the change process. Part of the change process involves being able to assist people in connecting their experiences of the past with the hope of the future. A good leader will help bring images, analogies, experiences, stories, and *people* from the past of the church into the present and into the future.

I remember well the day when I discovered it. The "it" was a tape recording of the church's senior pastor speaking, made about thirty years earlier. This particular pastor had been the pastor when the formerly "young marrieds" (who were now in their late fifties and early sixties) were in their most formidable years. That pastor had later died while serving (and so they named the prayer chapel after him . . . about the closest thing you get to being canonized in a Baptist church). In the recording the pastor shared a vision of church planting. I listened to it and made very specific notes. By acknowledging and reflecting that revered pastor's vision, I was able to cast a vision for church planting that honored both the past and the pastor. The church was able to maintain a heartbeat for church planting from that time forward!

Leadership in and through crisis is the reality of this size of ministry. Pastors who are called to this setting will experience the hand of God as they effectively lead their people to embrace their God-sizing potential for ministry. The challenge of the various crises will be met with health and life as people are affirmed for their gifts and the church family is focused to prioritize the Great Commission and Great Commandment in the strategy, structure, and systems of the ministry.

15.

Frying Pan Size 3: 400–800

Being a leader in a church serving more than four hundred people each weekend is difficult. It is difficult because the challenges faced by the leader and the church family are not only internal but also external. The external pressures are directly related to the expectations of those who are invited to the church or those who discover the church on their own. Once a church begins to have more than four hundred people, it is clearly too big to be small. But it is still too small to be big (at least until it reaches between eight hundred and one thousand in most places). That is why it is easy to call it an awkward-sized church. Most basic programs will be in place, but being able to deliver an excellent ministry is a significant challenge.

For leaders, the main issue is how to oversee and facilitate ministry leadership responsibilities that now clearly cannot be controlled by any one person or even any five people. The key word for this barrier is *delegation*, and the key principle is *structure*. The pastor must become a leader and focus time and energy on leading leaders (who in turn lead other leaders). Bill Easum said it well when he titled one of his books, *Sacred Cows Make Gourmet Burgers* (Abingdon, 1995). In a church of this size, leaders must be willing to kill some sacred cows (programs or ministries that have outlived their effectiveness) and organize ministry differently in order to reach more people for Christ.

I believe the two hundred barrier presents key leaders with a barrier of *heart*: do we have a vision to reach unchurched people? The fundamental question for churches at that level is whether they really care about people lost without Christ. The four hundred barrier presents a barrier of *behavior*: are we willing to change the way we do the ministry and life of the church in order to reach more people? Ministry at the four hundred barrier requires the pastor to raise up key team members who direct specific program ministries. For the pastor, this will often mean not only delegating responsibility but being secure enough to allow other leaders to have significant leadership influence without the micro-managing control that is natural to many pastoral leaders. This letting go will require developing structures to ensure that the church's mission, vision, values, and priorities stay in alignment. Pastors who lead these churches must learn to develop skills in managing people and projects.

Creating multiple program opportunities for people to connect in relationships and serve in ministry is essential to breaking through this barrier. Most churches understand the importance of having ministry on the weekends for worship, children, and students. Developing midweek ministries for discipleship, small groups, and local and global outreach will provide venues to connect people in relationships and give them an opportunity to serve. For many churches, the specific changes that are required at this level relate to bureaucracy. Will your church be willing to streamline the decision-making process and empower people to serve where they have passion and vision? During my time as a denominational leader, I interacted with a good number of churches that had long-established procedures and barriers that made serving in their church more difficult than getting top secret security clearance! Invariably when I asked leaders about those procedures and barriers, they were shocked at my perception—most often because they had not thought about the procedures for years.

Leaders in churches reaching more than four hundred people must prioritize equipping key leaders for ministry. Learning to delegate both power and authority is a fundamental part of this journey. It is a well-established maxim that when someone is given responsibility for a task, he or she should also be given authority to accomplish it. We understand this in our everyday work experience, but we violate it all the time in church. We ask people to accept responsibilities within the church but then don't give them the authority to accomplish the task. The biblical story of Nehemiah is instructive here. As soon as Nehemiah had a vision for rebuilding the wall, he knew that he not only needed to understand the vision (goal), but he also needed to gather the resources and necessary permissions. Thankfully, all Nehemiah had to do was to get permission and letters of credit from the king; he didn't have to file a single building permit or pass a single inspection!

Your church can reach more people for Christ, connect them in relationships, and equip them to serve if the senior leaders can surmount the barriers we have discussed in this chapter. Are you willing to change the way you do ministry and make decisions for the sake of engaging more and better-trained people in the process of ministry? God-sizing the impact of your church will dramatically increase if people are connected in relationships and they serve in ministry. It is a funny thing. The more you give ministry and leadership away, the more they grow, and your impact becomes God-sized.

There are some churches where God begins to move in such special ways that they reach beyond the eight hundred barrier. For those ministries, there are numerous difficult questions (and answers!) of evaluation that will determine their willingness to reach even more people for Christ. In my experience as a pastor and consultant, reaching more than two hundred people and reaching more than eight hundred to one thousand people are the two most gut-wrenching times in the life of a church, when hard questions have to be faced. Between four hundred and eight hundred people is the hardest size to manage. But to move beyond reaching eight hundred people each week is the most difficult barrier of evaluation and questioning that I have ever experienced. Many times people asked me, "Aren't we already reaching enough people? It is too crowded here already. Can't we stop growing?" I also remember having several conversations with staff leadership about the prospect of reaching more people, which simply meant more work.

Willow Creek Community Church in Chicago (www.willowcreek.org) recently released its REVEAL study (www.revealnow.com), a study of Willow Creek and several other churches that have committed to making disciples in the context of the local church. The study, conducted with a social science framework, concludes that if we are concerned about more than numbers, we must ask hard questions about what we do and what our activities produce. If your church is being blessed by God, is reaching more people, and is seeing changed lives for His glory, most likely, your church has asked and answered these tough questions:

- Do we *expect* that every human being can and should become a fully devoted follower of Jesus Christ?
- Are we *intentional* about doing all that we do in light of our size and our community environment?

- Are we *relevant* as we present the gospel? Are we addressing the longing that people have to feel understood, to understand, to belong to something, and to find hope?
- Are we *high quality* in what we present through teaching, worship, and training?
- Do we offer a broad range of attractive *choices* in a variety of areas?
- Do we *trust* our staff and lay leaders?
- Do we ask, "Was that a *good decision?*" instead of asking *who* made the decision?
- Do we operate from an *abundance model* in which "resource demands" are met by challenging people to find creative solutions?

In addition to asking tough questions about what we do and how we do it, churches that reach and influence more people for Christ often must change the way they organize and carry out leadership at the governance level. Governing boards in churches that are just arriving at this level tend to manage committees, which in turn coordinate volunteers. They also tend to protect physical assets of the church and possess status as nonclergy leaders. In order to make effective transition to the next level, the governing board of a church reaching more than eight hundred people will release the ministry to the staff (paid and volunteer) leaders of the ministry, who in turn lead growing teams of lay ministers. The governing board of the church then is largely responsible for establishing a climate of trust, authenticity, and support for the vision of the ministry. They help govern the life of the body in such a way as to make their primary focus the issue of health and not mechanics. There are a number of excellent resources on this subject. My personal favorites are *Direct Hit* by Paul Borden (Abingdon,

2006) and *Winning on Purpose* by John Kaiser (Abingdon, 2006).

An additional barrier for churches reaching and influencing more people is the area of staffing. The staff must make several transitions to move to the next level. The staff must move

- from provider to arranger of service
- from player to coach
- from solo star to team leader
- from privilege to accountability
- from area specialist to age-division generalist
- from personal ministry to delegation
- from committee *appraisal* (faithfulness) to *results* (fruitfulness)

Each change will require the leadership to provide structures and process to ensure that the staff and the other leaders receive feedback about their respective ministries. Many times, at these levels of growing impact, the question arises about the proper role of paid staff. In a larger, growing church, paid staff should do the following:

- Communicate mission, vision, and values.
- Manage the church's systems.
- Lead problem solving.
- Build relationships.
- Create new opportunities for ministry.
- Perceive the membership in terms of lay-led teams.
- Develop, disciple, and mentor new leaders.
- Train leaders in three areas: spiritual and relational vitality, core competencies, and change management.
- Have a clear method and curriculum for teaching leadership.

The challenges for this level of church are particularly onerous given that multiple issues can easily present themselves at any given time. Fortunately, in the latter part of the twentieth century and the first part of the twenty-first century, God has given us a number of healthy larger-church models that we can now both celebrate and observe after one or more decades of ministry. Utilizing other models for ministry as benchmarks, growing churches clarify their vision and focus their future in concert with God's hand upon their ministry. Adapting the principles you see in another larger-church ministry for ministry in your context is the challenge of leadership.

Breaking through barriers at all levels does not depend on the mechanics of ministry. Ultimately, the direction of a ministry rests completely in the hands of the Holy Spirit who calls, shapes, and gifts the members of the team. It is my prayer that your journey with God will result in the breaking of every barrier to growth and impact that God enables you to see and to challenge. Even now, I sense that you are beginning to believe God for greater impact than your church has ever experienced. Even now, I sense that you believe that God can change the trajectory of your church from stagnant and declining to growing and God-sizing in your community. Even now, I hear the walls falling down!

16.

So You Want to Start a God-Sized Church?

Maybe you are serving in a marketplace ministry, or maybe you've gotten a few years under your belt as an associate, and now that you've read all about a God-sized church, you'd like to start one. How would that work?

I believe that the ways in which God gives people dreams to start new churches are as varied as there are styles of churches. I have often coached church planters, and I am always amazed at the various ways God leads people to go about the task. Even now, I am coaching a church planter who came from a conservative evangelical background and has felt led to start a church with a sacramental and sometimes charismatic Anglican fellowship (see www.theamia.org/ for more information about this fascinating movement). Thankfully, there are many helpful resources for starting a church. Two of my favorites are *Launch* by Nelson Searcy and Kerrick Thomas (Regal Books, 2007) and *Planting Missional Churches* by Ed Stetzer (B & H, 2006).

I have written elsewhere (see www.pastorpreneur.com for additional information) about the eleven-step process that we have used with many church planters and in our own experience. I want to share them with you in the following pages. This is a tremendous step of faith for you and worthy of all the God-stirred excitement you feel. If you are up to the challenge of planting a church, you are in for the journey of a lifetime!

Step 1: Uphold a Clear, Well-processed, Prayed-for Vision

This vision has to be prayed through and shared in painstaking detail with successive groups of people who will join your team. Because God-sized churches reach large groups of people early on, it is essential to have a clear vision that you know comes from the throne of God (review chapters 2 and 6 for additional heartbeat challenges to developing the vision that God has for you). If you don't have a clear idea of what to do with the crowd when it comes, you will be in trouble!

There are some tremendous resources on the market to help you develop your action plan. Five of my favorites are *Purpose Driven Church Planting Materials* (http://www.saddlebackresources.com/en-US/Home.htm), *Dynamic Church Planting* (Paul Becker, www.dcpi.org), *Church Planter's Toolkit* (Bob Logan and Steve Ogne, Church Resource Ministries, www.crmleaders.org/), *Planting Thriving New Churches* (Ray Johnston, www.thriving churches.com), and as I mentioned a moment ago, *Launch* by Nelson Searcy and Kerrick Thomas (www.church leaderinsights.org).

Step 2: Lay Out an Aggressive Plan of Action, including a Fund-raising Plan

When I coach prospective church planters, they tend to underestimate the amount of money that will be required to successfully plant a God-sized church, and overestimate the amount that a denominational agency, mother church, or sponsor should be obligated to give them at launch. If you are the leader of a God-sized church, people whom you have influenced in ministry will support your vision. Raise funds from those who buy in to your vision based on God's working in their lives.

Fund-raising is a challenge for many pastors and church planters. Most pastors are hesitant to speak about money, and most church planters want someone else to raise the money while they do the ministry. But a God-sized–church leader must have the ability to cast a compelling vision and be the lead fund-raiser for the ministry. In our experience at CVC, we learned powerful lessons in this regard as God worked through our vision casting with various people and agencies.

The Apostle Paul certainly knew what it was to have a vision that came from God, yet he still required funds from ordinary people! Read some of these significant Bible passages about raising funds for ministry:

Acts 9:15-16
Romans 15:15-21
Galatians 1:15-24
Galatians 2:6-9
Ephesians 3:7-9
Philippians 4:15-17
Colossians 1:24-29
1 Timothy 2:7
2 Timothy 4:16-17

Step 3: Create a People Pathway for Assimilation

Assimilation at every level revolves around connecting people in relationships and in ministry service. I have found Rick Warren's model at Saddleback Community Church (www.saddlebackresources.com) to be the most helpful in our setting. In our ten-year history, we have morphed from the base path of the Purpose Driven model to a triangle and now an arc with the circles of involvement where our three primary environments are described (see chapter 7 for additional detail). We talk about our three environments as inviting, connecting, and serving (instead of asking people to remember four, five, or more things, we simplified to these three environments). Articulating a clear plan at the start helped people have confidence about where we were heading and connecting them in relationships and ministry.

The key process question in assimilation is this: can you take a new believer through the spiritual journey of discipleship to leadership? It is a critical question for all Christian ministries, and you must have your answer (at least in part) before your church launches. As I shared earlier (see chapter 4), our church has made many mistakes in the process of our growth and life, and after ten years, we are still working to get our systems and process in order.

Step 4: Make Your Church-planting Plans Flexible, and Be Open to Unexpected Opportunities

We had some great plans on paper! Some of them even worked. Others didn't. For example, we recorded thirteen sixty-second commercials for radio. We got no response. Direct mailing in our area was not nearly as effective as we had hoped. But we discovered some strategies that did fit our area. People in our community actually watch local public access television. Newspaper inserts reach 80 percent of all households in the area. The cost was substantially cheaper than direct mail, and people retained the inserts, sometimes for months.

There may be a God-sized ministry inside you that will be birthed sometime in the near future. My advice would be to use your "expectant" time to the fullest, reading books, consulting experts, and listening to birth stories. Those who have had a part in birthing a God-sized church or ministry usually don't need much prompting to tell their story. Become involved in a church-planting network where you can receive coaching, tools, and resources. (Two networks where I am personally involved are Growing Healthy Churches at www.growinghealthychurches.org and Thriving Churches at www.thrivingchurches.com.)

Step 5: Prayerfully Seek Godly Core Leaders and Key Ministry Leaders

Implosion is a critical danger to launching a God-sized church ministry. Churches that attract crowds and don't have the leadership base to effectively minister will be at a disadvantage from the start. Seeking godly core leaders as part of your launch team and cultivating a game plan for how the church will go public with specific ministries are necessary for a successful launch of the God-sized church. Here are several key roles for you to prayerfully pursue:

- a spiritually gifted leader and gifted communicator (may be one person or two)
- a worship leader who can help draw and connect other gifted musicians
- a children's ministry leader/facilitator
- a student ministry leader/facilitator

- a small-group coordinator for adults
- administratively gifted folks for office and ministry support

You could easily become discouraged by viewing this "dream" list. How many church plants fill every single position? The reality is that some people may overlap responsibilities and cover more than one area. But remember that no one person can fulfill all of them, and if you think you're the one, think again. Build a team of people around you, and go for it!

Step 6: Hold Preview Services 3 to 6 Months prior to Your Launch Service: Build Your Core to 100 Adults or More

Many church plants have benefited from the preview service strategy. Once each month (for a few months prior to the launch) the church offers a church service in the community. It's best to offer everything you would offer at a weekly service, such as children's classes and refreshments. This process was crucial to our church's early development. During your preview services, you may need to "borrow" key leaders from other churches (ideally a "mother church" or "partner church") in order to provide a basic children's ministry and worship experience. The church planter should speak here and provide a solid teaching that will meet real felt needs in the lives of those attending. (I focused on marriage and parenting in our preview services). During each of these services, you are looking to cast the vision for your church plant and praying that God will help you grow your leadership core. I believe in the power of strategic praying—so pray that God brings you the right leaders and that you see people come to know Christ at each preview service. At CVC, our experience was that people in our existing core got very excited when they experienced God's hand moving among us and the newer people who became part of the core could point to the preview service as the catalytic experience for them joining us in the journey.

Step 7: Engage People in Ministries, Discovery Classes, Small Groups, and Bible Studies

Providing easy on-ramps for people to join you in your ministry is essential at all times, but never more critical than at the early part of your new church life. At CVC, we offered "Discovery 101" (our new-attendee class) on the afternoon of our preview service, which gave an immediate opportunity for folks who were looking at the new church to hear more of our vision and plans. I would also challenge you to make it a high priority to connect people in relationships through small groups and service. My experience is that if people are challenged by the vision, connected in relationships through small groups, and serving in a ministry, they will be well attached to your church.

Step 8: Identify the Core Group as Your Launch Team; Create Job Descriptions and Prepare for Launch by Training Your Launch Team

My experience with church plants has been that insufficient leadership resources are a huge potential pitfall. I have personally witnessed many churches begin with a "bang" (an exciting launch) and end with a "whimper" (a final service) within the span of two or three years. I am convinced that one of the keys to preventing this cycle is to ensure that you have a large and broad leadership cohort at the beginning of your church life. Challenge people to know that they are personally critical to the success of the church launch. The Holy Spirit will draw many people to your church launch, but each person that comes is critical to God's plan. Ephesians 4:16-25 teaches us that each individual part contributes to the functioning of the whole body. During this launch phase of the church, the church planter needs to gather partners in ministry and be looking (again, with strategic prayer!) for gifted men and women to help lead the body that God is forming.

Step 9: Create Excellent Publicity, Especially Two Months before Launch

My brother Gene was the marketing whiz behind our church launch. He believes strongly in what I call "bread crumb" advertising. He builds a game plan where over a three- to six-week period, we build public interest and drive people to a specific response. Our theme, "The Next Great Day in History," moved people to focus on February 22, 1998. Then the second segment focused on the teaching series, "Winning Big in the Game of Life." Doing this publicity made some people mad; they were members of existing churches—even though we clearly were not targeting current church attendees. We like to say that during this period, we took the "flak" in order to build the "flock."

We involved our people in the process by giving them fold-over wallet-sized cards with the name of the church, topic of the teaching series, and the location and times of services, and then encouraging them to canvass neighborhoods and local businesses and hand out the cards.

The expectation is to create a buzz of activity in your area. When we launched, we think we created a big-event mentality. Not only is event evangelism in the center of our vision, but we believe that it is right for our area. The launch of your God-sized church is the most important event in its early life and will determine the trajectory of the next twelve to twenty-four months. We strongly believe that birth weight affects birth health. Although I recognize that some churches launch in a more organic way (utilizing small relational networks), what I provide here will be of great help to those establishing a church with a high attractional component.

Step 10: Plan a Super Launch and Go Public with the Key Things You'd Die For

You can't control everything. Mistakes happen. Weather may be stormy. People get sick. But you can decide what you are going to the wall for. CVC decided to focus on three things:

1. Relevant biblical messages
2. Upbeat contemporary music
3. Excellent children's ministry

These three program distinctives have remained our weekend focus to this day. If you were to go fishing, you would think about how fish think and what they like to eat, and make sure to offer the right bait. Church planting is about strategic penetration into an unreached culture, and it is crucial to think about what people really want in a church. My experience is that teaching, music, and children's ministry are the three key elements that most people look for, and that's *if* they decide to even visit a church. It is important that the teaching and music be high-quality, of course, since they make up the bulk of your worship experience. Children's ministry may seem peripheral to some church leaders, but it can make or break your new church start, especially given that many adults who have not attended church in recent years will start attending when they have children of their own.

Step 11: Go for It! Affirm Philippians 4:13 and Practice Continuous Improvement

Above all else, finish well! Consider these characteristics of those who have finished well, based on the research and experience of Paul D. Stanley and J. Robert Clinton:

1. They had perspective, which enabled them to focus.
2. They enjoyed intimacy with Christ and experienced repeated times of inner renewal.
3. They were disciplined in important areas of life.
4. They maintained a positive learning attitude all their lives.
5. They had a network of meaningful relationships and several important mentors during their lifetime.[1]

Expectant times are full of nervousness, stress, and a need for clear thinking. You may be in a significant "expectant" time of ministry now, or you may see one in your near future. Either way, my challenge to you is to seize the moment and learn as much as you can. When it happens, take a lot of pictures, record your memories, and share them with others who hope one day to birth their own exciting ministry.

God is sovereign. It is His church. You are accountable for gifts and resources He has entrusted to you. But He is the One who causes the growth. God will do way beyond your imagination, and you will see a thirty-, sixty-, or hundredfold return from the sowing of His seed. Spend time affirming your leadership team. Be a positive person from the platform, and practice continuous improvement. Build a culture of affirmation and expectation, and go for it! If there is a God-sizing vision within you, He will help you build the ministry that He has placed inside your heart and mind.

17.

The Ripple Effect: "Get out of Line—It's Worth It!"

Kim and Carol found us when we were not even an official church. They were lapsed Lutherans who had seen an advertisement for an event we did a few weeks earlier and decided to check us out after the big event. We were meeting in a casino ballroom, forming a core group for the eventual church launch. On the day they attended, our core group was doing its first baptism of twelve people. The baptism took place in the back hallway of the casino ballroom in a hot tub purchased at a garage sale. We had filled it with water directly from the hot water heater, via one hundred fifty feet of garden hose trailing down the hallway and into the kitchen, so steam rose in thick swirls as it hit the air from the twelve-degree weather outside, racing its way up the stairwell from a door that someone had left open on the first floor. Kim's response to all this? "Any group of people this crazy for God are people I want to be around."

About two years later, with their family growing in faith, one of Kim and Carol's daughters invited her friend Casey to be part of a children's choir we started. After a few weeks of Casey's participation in the choir, her parents, Curt and Laura, thought they better find out what this church was all about. Curt was a nonbelieving

Catholic, and Laura was a lapsed Baptist. On the way out after the service, Curt headed toward me with a determined look. I thought, *Oh, man, I'm in trouble.* What I didn't tell you is that Curt is a former NFL lineman. He's big! He hugged me (I still thought I was going to die) without saying anything and walked out the door. The second weekend they attended, he came to me with that same look, but this time with tears in his eyes, and he said that he had "prayed the prayer" and asked Christ into his life. Laura rededicated her life to Christ as well.

Those decisions were made about seven years ago. Today Curt and Laura are still active at CVC and have invited many other friends who have made decisions for Christ. Curt has been involved in developing sports ministry, video for weekend services and special projects, and many other forms of outreach. Laura has served in our communications ministry for the past several years and as our communications director. Both continue to inspire lives every week for the cause of Christ.

In one monologue Jeff Foxworthy described seeing an unusual person at a county fair and then told his friends to "get out of line, it's worth it!" Well, I believe that many churches are patiently standing in line, waiting for the same result and the same power that they have always expected and experienced. God wants us to "get out of line" and pursue a God-sized church with all the risks and challenges that will bring.

So, is it worth it? Is it worth all the risk, all the challenge, all the uncertainty? Yes! The power of God to change a life never grows old. Mike Breaux wrote the book *Making Ripples* (Zondervan, 2007) based on a sermon he preached. When I first heard the sermon, Mike shared the wonderful image of a pebble dropping in a pond, sending ripples from the point of initial impact outward. The kingdom of God works the same way. The power of God touches a life. Then that life touches another life and another life, and the kingdom of God takes root in our everyday lives as we learn to live in right relationship with Jesus Christ and with one another.

I believe in the power of God to change not only a human life but also a church. A church that becomes a God-sized church will influence its community in ways that are ultimately measurable only in eternity. While I believe this with all my heart, the truth is that the challenges are huge. I agree with Robert Lewis when he says:

> As the church engages a third millennium, it . . . looks across a terrifying—and ever-widening—chasm:
> Between first-century authority and postmodern skepticism;
> Between a bold proclamation of God's love and unmet human needs;
> Between the selfless vision of Christ and the self-obsessed reality of our world;
> Between the truth of God's laws and the moral compromise of our culture;
> Between those who believe and those who don't.[1]

As church leaders, we simply must face that chasm with an unshakable conviction that the church is the hope of the world when we present the good news of Christ in relevant and accessible ways to men and women whose hearts are far from Him. Robert Lewis also challenges church leaders to become "bridge builders" and connect the church with the community. Lewis knows that a bridge builder is about making a God-sized impact in the world through transformed and mobilized people: "A 'bridge builder' has a vision to raise the lifestyle standards of his people and move his church off its island setting into a city or community. He crafts strategy, builds structure, and measures success, not in terms of size or programming, but in terms of authentic witness, influence, and impact in the community at large." A bridge builder instinctively knows that "a church's health is measured by its sending capacity, not its seating capacity."[2]

This book, *God-Size Your Church*, has been an invitation to dream big dreams for God—and to begin living and leading in the land of those dreams, watching them become realities. There are formidable dangers in the land, to be sure, and they are not to be trifled with. But neither are they to be overly feared. He who called you is faithful; ultimately, there is no safer or more joyful place to live than in the center of God's big dream for you.

We will continue to live out and breathe the story that God is writing at Carson Valley Christian Center. If God is birthing in you a heartbeat for a God-sized ministry, then we'd love to hear from you! If you go through the process of starting a high-impact church, we'd love to hear the story of how God works in your vision to produce a harvest that is thirty-, sixty-, or a hundredfold. You may write me at the following address: Dr. John Jackson, Carson Valley Christian Center, 1095 Stephanie Way, Minden, Nevada 89423.

Included in the appendix are documents that might be helpful for your ministry. Some of them are from the early days in our church life and represent the very basics when we started the church, while others represent very recent realities. We try to keep growing and improving our ministry. However, if you can use these resources and improve them for other church planters and leaders, please do so and share the improved versions with us!

We are yours for the kingdom. Seeing a life change, transforming a family, and inspiring a community for the cause of Christ are worth the investment of your life. A God-sized church will change lives for all eternity . . . including yours!

Appendix

Bylaws of the Carson Valley Christian Center, Inc.

This church shall be known as the Carson Valley Christian Center, incorporated under the laws of the State of Nevada. (We have chosen to use the masculine pronoun throughout the doctrinal section of this document for ease of language, but our intent is to describe both genders, not the male gender exclusively.)

Purpose

Carson Valley Christian Center (CVC) exists to see non-Christians become disciples of Jesus Christ.

Carson Valley Christian Center will dynamically . . .

. . . exalt Jesus, the Light of the World

. . . equip believers to walk in the Light

. . . encourage one another to share the Light

Statement of Faith

Scripture

We believe that the Bible is the Word of God, fully inspired and without error in the original manuscripts, written under the inspiration of the Holy Spirit, and that it has supreme authority in all matters of faith and conduct (2 Timothy 3:16-17).

The Trinity

We believe that there is one living God, and that He has revealed Himself in three distinct persons: God the Father, God the Son, and God the Holy Spirit (Titus 3:4-6).

a) God the Father: We believe in God the Father: an infinite, personal spirit, perfect in holiness, wisdom, power, and love. We believe that He concerns Himself mercifully in the affairs of men, and that He saves from sin and death all who come to Him through Jesus Christ.

b) God the Son: We believe that Jesus Christ is fully God and fully man. He is eternal and shares all of the attributes of deity with the Father and the Holy Spirit, as God's only begotten Son. He was conceived by the Holy Spirit to be born of a virgin, Mary. We believe in His virgin birth, sinless life, miracles, and teachings. We believe in His substitutionary atoning death, bodily resurrection, ascension into Heaven, perpetual intercession for His people, and personal, visible return to earth.

c) God the Holy Spirit: We believe that the Holy Spirit is a person and shares all the attributes of deity with the Father and the Son. He came forth from the Father and the Son to convict the world of sin, righteousness, and judgment, and to regenerate, sanctify, and empower all who believe in Jesus Christ, and that He is an abiding Helper, Teacher, and Guide.

Salvation

We believe that all men are sinners by nature and by choice and are, therefore, deserving of eternal condemnation. We believe that those who repent of their sins and trust in Jesus Christ as Lord and Savior are regenerated and become children of God by the Holy Spirit (John 1:12; Romans 5:6-8).

The Church

We believe that the Church is the Body of Christ, of which Christ is the Head. It consists of all regenerated persons. We believe in local churches as visible manifestations of the invisible Body of Christ, the Church Universal. We believe that God has given the task of evangelism of the world to the Church under the direction of the Holy Spirit and the Word of God (Acts 1:8; 1 Corinthians 12:12-14; Ephesians 1:22).

Christian Living

We believe that a Christian should live for the glory of God and the well-being of others. Believers are called to live holy and godly lives (1 Corinthians 10:31; 1 Peter 1:5-6; Matthew 22:37-40).

Ordinances

We believe that ordinances of the New Testament church are communion (the Lord's Supper) and water baptism for believers by immersion as a public act of confession of faith (Acts 8:36-39; 1 Corinthians 11:23-26).

Last Things

We believe in the personal and visible return of the Lord Jesus Christ to earth and the establishment of His kingdom. We believe in the resurrection of the body, the final judgment, the eternal joy of the righteous, and the endless suffering and separation of the lost (Acts 1:11; Isaiah 9:6-7; 2 Peter 3:7; John 3:16).

Christian Liberties

We believe in the personal lordship of Christ over individual believers. Each believer must give account for himself to Christ. Therefore, in matters not strictly defined in Scripture, convictions of one should not be imposed on others (Romans 14).

Article 1: Membership

Section 1: Membership and Requirements

Membership in the church family is open to those who meet the following requirements:

a) Profession of faith in Jesus Christ as Savior and Lord.

b) Completion of membership class requirements as outlined in church ministry documents.

A list of members who are actively participating in church ministries will be maintained.

Section 2: Dismissals

Membership may be terminated in the following ways:

a) Member initiates request for membership termination.

b) The Elders may remove a person's name from membership after appropriate efforts to restore fellowship and participation have failed. There shall be no time limit, but shall be up to the discretion and good judgment of the Elders.

c) The Elders may dismiss a member as part of a disciplinary action.

Section 3: Annual Meeting

There may be an annual meeting of the membership. The place, date, and time of the annual meeting will be announced in public worship or in print two weeks prior to the meeting. The annual meeting, when held, will be for the purpose of consideration of any ministry matters appropriate for the membership to consider or modification of the Bylaws.

Article 2: Government

Section 1: The Headship of Christ

The government of CVC will seek to maintain the lordship and direction of Jesus Christ as the Head of this Body. Those in authority will continually seek His mind and His will, through His Spirit and His Word in all actions and decisions.

Section 2: The Board of Directors

The Accountability Team will serve as the corporate Board of Directors of the church. As such they will seek to support the ministry of the church by precept and example under the lordship of Christ and through the leadership of the Pastor. They will pray together regularly and review the progress of the ministry. They will gather together for prayer and counsel on a regular basis, at least monthly. Members of the Accountability Team will be selected by a majority vote of the members then serving.

Subject to the limitations of the Articles of Incorporation, other sections of the Bylaws, and of Nevada law, all corporate powers of the corporation shall be exercised by or under the authority of, and the business and governance affairs of the corporation will be managed by the Directors. Without limiting their general authority, the Directors shall have the following authority:

a) To select and remove all other officers, agents, and employees of the corporation; prescribe such powers and duties for them as may or may not be inconsistent with the law, the Articles of Incorporation, or the Bylaws and fix their compensation.

b) To conduct, manage, and control the activities and business of the corporation; and to make rules and policies not inconsistent with the law, Articles of Incorporation, or the Bylaws.

c) To borrow money and incur indebtedness for the purposes of the corporation, and for that purpose to authorize to be executed and delivered, in the corporate name, promissory notes, bonds, debentures, deeds of trust, mortgages, pledges, or other evidences of debt and securities.

Section 3: Elders

In addition to Directors, the church will have a Pastoral Staff who serve as the Elders of the church. These men will meet biblical qualifications and are responsible to shepherd the spiritual health of the church family.

To be selected as an Elder, a man must meet the qualifications outlined in Scripture in 1 Timothy 3:1-7 and Titus 1:5-9.

There will be a minimum of at least two and no more than fifteen Elders. Additional Elders may be added by the procedure described below. Elders will be nominated by the Pastor and a majority vote of the Elders then serving.

An Elder, other than the Pastor, may be removed from office by the vote of a majority of the Elders then serving. The Pastor may only be removed by a two-thirds (2/3) majority vote of the voting membership of the church present at a meeting called in accordance with Article 4.

Article 3: Officers of the Church

Section 1: Officers

The officers of this corporation will be a President, may include a Vice President, and a Secretary and Treasurer. The Directors may also appoint other officers as they may deem necessary. No person, other than the President, may hold more than one office.

Section 2: Election

The Directors shall elect by simple majority vote the officers of the corporation from their number at the first meeting of each year. The term of office is to be one year, or until their successors are elected and qualified.

Section 3: President (Pastor)

Subject to ratification of the Board of Directors, the President shall have general supervision, direction, and control of the business and activities of the corporation. He shall be responsible for the presidency of all meetings of the membership, Elders, Directors, and shall have other powers and duties as may be prescribed from time to time by the Directors.

The primary ministries of the Pastor are to be the lead visionary, teacher, and equipper. He will give himself to the ministry of the Word and prayer. He will teach, guide, and lead the church to fulfill the vision for ministry that God has entrusted to him and to this Body. As President, he also serves as the Chief Executive Officer of the Corporation and Chair of the Elders. He is responsible to supervise and provide direction for any other staff and/or ministries of the church.

In the event of a vacancy in the office of President (Pastor), the Elders shall develop a committee to search for a successor Pastor. Once the right candidate is found (either within the Body or from outside candidates), the candidate will be presented to the church membership. A 75 percent vote of those voting members present (with at least a quorum of 30 percent of the voting membership present) will be required to elect a new President.

The Pastor is to be compensated by written agreement with the Directors. Compensation, benefits, and expenses provided will include (as God supplies the resources): housing allowance, salary, health insurance, retirement, continuing education, and other reasonable ministry expenses. The written agreement is to be reviewed no less than annually.

If a termination of the Pastor is to be considered, it requires the call of at least two Elders to initiate a meeting of the Elders. The meeting shall be called in accordance with the procedure for establishing a special meeting. Should three-fourths (3/4) of the Elders then serving concur that the Pastor should terminate his pastoral leadership of the church, the matter will be brought before the voting membership at a duly called meeting. A three-quarters (3/4) majority of the voting membership (with a quorum of 30 percent of the voting membership present) will be required to terminate the pastoral ministry.

Section 4: Other Ministerial or Support Staff

The Pastor may present other ministerial or support staff to lead the ministry to the Accountability Team for their advice and consent. Each staff person so presented will have a job description containing duties and compensation reviewed by the Accountability Team. All staff members serve under the Pastor's direction and supervision, and at his pleasure.

Section 5: Vice President

In the absence or disability of the President, if the organization has a Vice President, the Vice President shall perform temporarily all the duties of the President, and in so acting shall have all the powers of the President until the Directors take action on the vacancy. The Vice President may have such other powers and perform other duties as may be prescribed from time to time by the Directors.

Section 6: Secretary

The Secretary shall keep a full and complete record of all the proceedings of the Directors; shall keep the seal of the corporation and affix it to such papers as may be required in the regular course of business; shall make services of such notices as may be necessary or proper; shall supervise the keeping of records of the corporation; and may have other such duties as prescribed by the Directors.

Section 7: Treasurer

The Treasurer shall receive and safely keep all funds of the corporation and deposit them in the bank or banks that may be designated by the Directors through the administrative staff of the church. Financial procedures, as indicated in these Bylaws or in policies adopted by the Directors, shall be followed in the disbursement of funds.

Article 4: Financial Support and Fiscal Year

This church shall operate on a calendar year from January 1 through December 31. This church shall be supported through the tithes and offerings of its members and friends.

Article 5: Miscellaneous

Section 1: Execution of Documents

The Directors may authorize by majority vote any officer or officers, agent or agents, to enter into any contract or execute any instrument in the name of, and on behalf of the church and such authority may be general or confined to specific instances. Unless so authorized, no officer, agent, or other person shall have any power or authority to bind the church by any contract or engagement or to pledge its credit or to render it liable for any purpose or to any amount.

Section 2: Inspection of Bylaws

The church shall keep in its principal office the original or a copy of its Articles of Incorporation and Bylaws, as amended to date, certified by the Secretary, which shall be open to inspection by the members at all reasonable times during the office hours.

Section 3: Construction of Definitions

Unless the context otherwise requires, the general provisions, rules of construction, and definitions contained in the Nevada Nonprofit Corporation Law shall govern the construction of these Bylaws.

Section 4: Rules of Order

The rules contained in Robert's Rules of Order, as most recently revised, shall be the general guide to govern all business and/or Board meetings of the church, except in instances of conflict between said Rules of Order and the Articles of Incorporation and Bylaws of the church or provisions of law.

Section 5: Dissolution and Nonprofit Status

The property of this corporation is irrevocably dedicated to religious purposes and no part of the net income or assets of the organization shall ever inure to the benefit of any Director, officer, or member thereof or to the benefit of any private person.

The Directors shall make a recommendation regarding dissolution to the membership; said action to be approved by a two-thirds (2/3) vote of the membership. On the dissolution or winding up of the corporation, its assets remaining after payment of, or provision for payment of, all debts and liabilities of this corporation, shall be distributed to a nonprofit fund, foundation, or corporation which is organized and operated exclusively for religious purposes and which has established its tax-exempt status under section 501(c)3 of the Internal Revenue Code.

Section 6: Liability

No officer, Director, Elder, or representative appointed by this church shall be personally or individually liable for any error, mistake, act of omission for, or on behalf of this church, occurring in the scope of his or her duty as such officer, Director, Elder, or representative, excepting only for his or her own willful misconduct or violation of law.

Article 6: Amendment of Bylaws

These Bylaws may be amended or repealed and new Bylaws adopted by the membership of the church at a properly called meeting. Amendments shall be provided to the membership upon recommendation to the Accountability Team. Adoption of amendments or new Bylaws shall require a three-fourths (3/4) vote of the membership.

Ministry Program Leaders Expectations (updated 5/07)

Periodically it is important to clarify basic expectations for our ministry together. I have written elsewhere about how subministries (basically, everything but the weekend service) get developed and led with excellence. For those of you who give leadership within a ministry area, I thought you should also know the five key things that I expect every ministry area to do:

1. Understand and communicate the CVC mission and vision. Our mission is "Reaching unchurched people to become disciples of Jesus Christ," and our vision is "The spiritual transformation of Northern Nevada and the Mountain West through the power of Jesus Christ." *Nothing* at CVC (including me!!) is above that mission and vision . . . the vision drives and directs *everything* at CVC. If that vision is not being fulfilled through an activity, then kill it and get going with something that does fulfill the vision.

2. Create an environment where the vision can be fulfilled. We have three primary kinds of environments at CVC . . . *inviting environments* where people can

experience God and come to know Christ as Savior and where we can invite and bring our friends to meet Christ, *connecting environments* where people can connect their hearts to God and to one another in authentic relationships, and *serving environments* where people can discover and utilize their SHAPE (Spiritual Gifts, Heart/Passion, Ability, Personality, Experiences) for serving on campus, in the community, and in the world.

3. Make sure that ours is an environment where people are counted because people count! End of discussion. I can't live with subministry environments where we don't know who participates, whether they are consistent in attending, or whether we've seen them in the last few weeks (or months!). Someday, we'll even get to the place where we can do a good job with "knowing" the crowd/curious on the weekends. But the congregation, connected, and core *must* be counted. See definitions below.

4. Foster an environment where relationship values get lived out. LifeTeams, in all their varied forms, simply means that we create an environment where people are known, challenged to grow, and healthy spiritual habits are encouraged. In the end, I know with absolute certainty that if our people don't develop a biblical foundation/worldview, experience authentic relationships, and discover their SHAPE, then they will *not* be "fruit that remains . . . ," and we will have failed in our vision to create disciples.

5. Lead a team of people who are doing ministry, leaders of others who are doing ministry, and developing leaders of leaders. Over time, CVC will rise or fall based on leadership . . . because everything rises and falls on leadership! I've often used the "carpenter, contractor, architect" analogy with staff members. Each ministry area should have "first serve" places where people can step in and do *something* to help them connect and begin

to find their gifts (carpenters). Every ministry should be developing leaders who can oversee others doing the ministry (contractors). Each ministry should also be passionate about identifying, growing, and releasing ministry to high-capacity volunteers and equipping leaders who are leaders of leaders (architects).

CVC People-tracking Definitions (5/07)

Community . . . Anyone we've had contact with and who gave us his or her name and address. We cull this list once a year.

Curious . . . These are folks who are periodic attendees at CVC, but to our knowledge have made no commitment to Christ and are not plugged into anything at CVC.

Congregation . . . These are folks who are attendees at CVC, but other than participating in some activities are not plugged into a small group or serving at CVC.

Connected . . . These are members and regular attendees who are involved in a small group and/or are serving in ministry at CVC, with an understanding of the mission/vision/values of CVC. To the best of our knowledge they are striving to lead a Christ-centered, biblically grounded, heart-sensitive life.

Core . . . These are members (people who have completed 101-201-301) who are committed to the mission/vision/values of CVC and can communicate those to others, are involved in a small group, are serving in a ministry role, and striving to live a Christ-centered, biblically grounded, heart-sensitive life.

CVC Values

1. Evangelism occurs primarily in relational contexts in family, work, neighborhood, and community

settings and secondarily in outreach events that are easily accessible to seekers.

2. God's Word is consistently and relevantly taught in corporate worship, small groups, classes, personal discipleship, and through creative activities.

3. Performing arts are honored and utilized to the glory of God in a fashion relevant and accessible to seekers.

4. Community life in the church family is so honored that division and gossip are confronted quickly, clearly, and resolved in accordance with biblical principles of fellowship and conflict resolution.

5. Spiritual gifts discovery and utilization are essential aspects of discipleship for every believer.

6. Ministry programs and activities are started, led, and grown by gifted men and women from the church family.

7. Support ministries are led by people with serving gifts. These people are regularly honored and affirmed.

8. Pastoral staff model ministry values of team, affirmation, and excellence through their teaching and relating with the church family.

9. We honor those God has gifted and called to authority. Those in authority exercise their leadership with humility and grace as servant-leaders.

10. Stewardship of God's financial resources is practiced, modeled, and taught with passion and clarity.

Notes

2. God-Size Your Church by Dreaming God-Sized Dreams

1. *Purpose-Driven Church*, 43.
2. George Barna, *The Second Coming of the Church* (Nashville: Word, 2001), 1.
3. American Society for Church Growth, www.ascg.org/index. htm.

3. Is God-Sizing a Biblical Concept?

1. C. Peter Wagner, presentation at Fuller Theological Seminary, circa 1983.
2. See www.perrynoble.com.
3. Ed Young Jr., www.creativepastors.com.
4. Walt Kallestad, *Turning Your Church Inside Out* (Minneapolis Augsburg Press, 2001), 12.

5. Four Ingredients to God-Sizing Your Church

1. See www.enewhope.org, Willow Creek Leadership Summit, 2002.

6. God-Size Your Vision

1. Gary McIntosh and Glen Martin, *Finding Them, Keeping Them* (Nashville: Broadman Press, 1992), 22.

7. God-Size Your Environments

1. Gary McIntosh and Glen Martin, *Finding Them, Keeping Them* (Nashville: Broadman Press, 1992), 132.

9. God-Size Your Leaders

1. Peter F. Drucker in the foreword of *The Leader of the Future: New Visions, Strategies, and Practices for the Next Era*, ed. Frances Hesselbein, Marshall Goldsmith, Richard Beckhard (San Francisco: Jossey-Bass, 1997), xiii.

10. Barriers to God-Sizing: Your Frying Pan Is Too Small!

1. Lyle E. Schaller, *The Very Large Church* (Nashville: Abingdon Press, 2000), 107.

11. Leadership Barriers, Part 1

1. Larry Osborne, *The Unity Factor* (Carol Stream, Ill.: CTI, 1989), 85.

12. Leadership Barriers, Part 2

1. *Your Church Has Real Possibilities* (Ventura, Calif. Regal Books, 1974), 4.
2. Corrie Ten Boom, *The Hiding Place* (Ada, Mich.: Chosen Books, 1984), 74.
3. Gary McIntosh and Glen Martin, *Finding Them, Keeping Them: Effective Strategies for Evangelism and Assimilation in the Local Church* (Nashville: B & H Publishing Group, 1991), 9.

13. Frying Pan Size 1: Under 200

1. Dr. Mark Chaves et al., "The National Congregations Study: Background, Methods, and Selected Results," *Journal for the Scientific Study of Religion* 38 (1999): 458-76.

14. Frying Pan Size 2: 200–400

1. David Olson, *The American Church in Crisis* (Grand Rapids: Zondervan, 2008).

16. So You Want to Start a God-Sized Church?

1. Paul D. Stanley and J. Robert Clinton, *Connecting: The Mentoring Relationships You Need to Succeed in Life.* Used by permission of NavPress. Copyright 1992, all rights reserved. www.navpress.com.

17. The Ripple Effect: "Get Out of Line—It's Worth It!"

1. Robert Lewis, *The Church of Irresistible Influence* (Grand Rapids: Zondervan, 2001), 23.
2. Ibid., 177.

Bibliography

Barna, George. *The Second Coming of the Church*. Nashville: Word, 2001.

Borden, Paul. *Hit the Bullseye*. Nashville: Abingdon Press, 2003.

————. *Direct Hit*. Nashville: Abingdon Press, 2006.

Breaux, Mike. *Making Ripples*. Grand Rapids: Zondervan, 2007.

Collins, Jim. *Good to Great*. New York: HarperBusiness, 2001.

Cordeiro, Wayne. *Doing Church as a Team*. Ventura, Calif.: Regal Books, 2004.

Easum, Bill. *Sacred Cows Make Gourmet Burgers*. Nashville: Abingdon Press, 1995.

George, Carl, and Warren Bird. *How to Break Growth Barriers*. Grand Rapids: Baker Press, 1993.

Jackson, John. *PastorPreneur*. VisionQuest Ministries, 2003.

Jackson, John and Lorraine Bossé-Smith. *Leveraging Your Leadership Style*. Nashville: Abingdon Press, 2006.

Kaiser, John. *Winning on Purpose*. Nashville: Abingdon Press, 2006.

Kallestad, Walt. *Turn Your Church Inside Out*. Minneapolis: Augsburg Fortress Press, 2001.

Lewis, Robert. *The Church of Irresistible Influence*. Grand Rapids: Zondervan, 2001.

Maxwell, John. *21 Irrefutable Laws of Leadership*. Nashville: Thomas Nelson Publishers, 1999.

McIntosh, Gary, and Glen Martin. *Finding Them, Keeping Them: Effective Strategies for Evangelism and Assimilation in the Local Church*. Nashville: B & H Publishing Group, 1991.

Olson, David. *The American Church in Crisis*. Grand Rapids: Zondervan, 2008.

O'Neill, Tip. *All Politics Is Local*. Holbrook, Mass.: Adams Media Corporation, 1995.

Osborne, Larry. *The Unity Factor*. Owl's Nest Publishing, 1989.

Rusaw, Rick, and Eric Swanson. *The Externally Focused Church*. Loveland, Colo.: Group, 2004.

Schaller, Lyle. *The Very Large Church*. Nashville: Abingdon Press, 2000.

Searcy, Nelson, and Jennifer Dykes Henson. *Fusion: Integrating Newcomers into the Life of Your Church*. Ventura, California: Regal Books, 2008.

Searcy, Nelson, and Kerrick Thomas. *Launch*. Ventura, California: Regal Books, 2007.

Stanley, Paul, and Robert Clinton. *Connecting: The Mentoring Relationships You Need to Succeed in Life*. Colorado Springs, Colo.: NavPress, 2006.

Stetzer, Ed. *Planting Missional Churches*. Nashville: B & H Publishers, 2006.

Sullivan, Bill. *New Perspectives on Breaking the 200 Barrier*. Kansas City, Mo.: Beacon Hill Press of Kansas City, 2005.

Ten Boom, Corrie. *The Hiding Place*. Washington Depot, Conn.: Chosen Books, 1984.

Tichy, Noel. *The Leadership Engine*. New York: Harper Business, 2002.

Toffler, Alvin. *Future Shock*. New York: Random House, 1970.

Warren, Rick. *The Purpose-Driven Church*. Grand Rapids: Zondervan, 1995.